When all the Trees were Green

WHEN ALL THE TREES WERE GREEN

AN EARTHY STORY OF VILLAGE LIFE

Jack Ivester Lloyd

Kineton: The Roundwood Press
1973

Jack Ivester Lloyd has also written

Joey the Pony (1938)
Scrap the Terrier (1938)
Flash the Gipsy Dog (1939)
Full Cry (1939)
The People of the Valley (1943)
Adventures of Tip the Terrier (1947)
Johnny Rides Out (1948)
Well Ridden (1949)
Moonmaiden's Treasure (1950)
Rabbiting and Ferreting (1950) (*In collaboration with E. S. Samuel*)
Ginger (1951)
Riders of the Heath (1951)
Come Hunting (1952)
Beagling (1954)
Happy the Hare (1960)
Otter's Path (1961)
Beaglers (1971)
Hounds of Britain (1973)

First published in 1973 by
The Roundwood Press (Publishers) Limited,
Kineton, Warwick, England

SBN 900093 42 0

Set in 'Monotype' Van Dijck series 203, and printed by
Gordon Norwood at The Roundwood Press, Kineton
in the County of Warwick, England
and bound by Eric Neal, Welford, Rugby

Made and printed in Great Britain

Contents

When all the world is young, lad,
And all the trees are green;
And every goose a swan, lad,
And every lass a queen;
Then hey for boot and horse, lad,
And round the world away;
Young blood must have its course, lad,
And every dog his day.

CHARLES KINGSLEY

CHAPTER ONE

Background

MINE WAS A happy childhood. I led the life of a normal, healthy village boy in the days when every wood was a place of dark mystery, alive with birds and animals and watched over by grim gamekeepers whose presence added to the thrill of penetrating their domains. Where primroses and bluebells flowered and hazel nuts in their season were waiting to be shaken to the ground.

Blue and white violets bloomed under straggling hedgerows and alongside others which had been 'cut and laid', tributes to the hands and brains of labourers who had learned their skill from their fathers, and who in turn hoped to pass them on to their own sons. Few were able to do so. For it was those same sons who, a short while later, left their plough teams, laid down their fagging hooks and betook themselves to the village constable.

"Please sir," said these lads, dressed in their Sunday suits and with their cheeks scrubbed to the rosiness of a hollyberry. "Please sir, will you tell us how we can serve our King and Country?"

He told the boys and, on my way back from school, I passed them, marching raggedly towards the nearest recruiting centre. I saw very few of them ever again. But that took place after my story ends, though not long after. My story is set in the times immediately before the outbreak of the First World War.

Then in the fields between those quick hedgerows, there grew wild thyme, Dutch clover, daisies to be picked and threaded into chains, not only by the girls but quite unashamedly by some of the boys. There was sorrel too, the leaves of which could be eaten although they had a bitter flavour. Quaker grass waved seeds in the wind. Wild bees made nests from which, if you were quick, you could snatch a small comb and suck out the honey.

Field and bank voles, 'hogmice,' had their burrows not as deep nor of such length as those of moles. If you knew how, you could find these burrows and poke out the snubnosed inmates with a willow wand. Overhead, on quivering wings, the occasional kestrel waited and, at dusk, big, white, ghostlike owls floated above the tops of the hedges where orange-chested fieldmice foraged for food.

My companions had an instinct for ferreting out any living creature, especially if it could be put in the pot. For most of them were descended from many generations of poachers. Their reactions to the sight of a wild rabbit were much the same as those of the terrier I kept in later years. They tolerated my presence on poaching and birdnesting expeditions though I can never think why, when my interests were more often in the creatures themselves than in their capture.

What those companions could never understand was why, after some particularly exciting adventure, I would go home and relate it in full detail to my parents. As one of them said when he learned this, "If *I* told our mum what I'd done, she'd tell our dad when he came home and he'd give me a clip round the ear-'ole."

I was fortunate in having parents who could forgive almost anything provided it made them laugh. Both had a terrific sense of humour but, while my father's was of a Rabelaisian nature, Ma's was often inclined to be impish, a not uncommon trait in small, dark-haired women. He was big, inclining to fat, in spite of the exercise he took with his beagles, and, generally, easy going. Dad took a lot of upsetting but when he *was* uspet he became, as Ma once told her sister, Aunt Ede, "like a raving bull." He would storm around, tearing his rather scanty crop of red hair and cursing. Owing possibly to seafaring forefathers, he was, like Shakespeare's soldier, "full of strange oaths" which, because I could not understand them, fascinated me. But he was seldom actually violent and the storm would end when he had stamped off to his studio, slammed the door behind him and found consolation in his charcoal and paint.

In the days which I am trying to describe, my father was beginning to make a reasonable living as an artist. I don't think he was ever outstanding in his colour work but his draughtsmanship was superb. With a few strokes of a pencil or charcoal stick he could convey the form and action of a horse, a hound or any other of the animals of which he was so fond.

I suppose my father was really a countryman by adoption which may account for his enthusiasm; there are few firmer believers than the converts. Ma, however, was a country-woman born and reared. The daughter of a farmer and butcher, she had learned to ride and drive a pony almost as soon as she could walk and was possessed of a quick, often barbed wit.

Both my parents were members of large families so it was rather surprising that I should be an only child. When very young, I had a serious illness which earned me fame in the village. "Prayed for in church, he were!" When I recovered, I was cossetted until a sensible family doctor pointed out that this was being overdone.

"What you mean, Doctor," my father said, "is that we're mollycoddling the boy?"

"That is exactly what I am hinting at."

"Then it would be better if he were to be turned out rough?" my father grinned with delight as he asked the question. And that was when country life really started for me. From then onwards I ran, roamed and occasionally fought with the other boisterous young savages whose fathers were 'on the land' or working at other mainly outdoor occupations. I acquired the accent and dialect of that corner of England where the three counties of Buckinghamshire, Bedfordshire and Northamptonshire run close together. This is my native tongue into which I still lapse when tired or excited.

The village itself was unique in those days in that it did not have a squire. There was a manor house but, apart from a garden, it had no land attached. This may have partly accounted for the almost complete lack of discipline and respect for authority, a spirit that produced a collection of independent individuals. During the whole of my joyous life there I don't think I ever saw a forelock pulled.

When the members of some well-meaning organisation toured the district in a horse-brake with the idea of suggesting improvements, they were received in the other villages with due respect. The little boys, lined up in their best suits and with freshly sponged celluloid collars, touched their foreheads. Their sisters, in starched pinafores, curtsied and proffered bunches of flowers.

This, or something similar, happened in every village visited by that band of do-gooders, every one, until they came to ours. Here the girls gave expressionless, insolent stares and a few put out long pink tongues. As for the boys, they picked up loose stones, of which there was a plentiful supply on the street, and threw them with alarming accuracy, safe in the knowledge that the village policeman had gone out to a distant farm about a gun licence.

The brake driver whipped up his pair of nags and drove out of the village while his passengers, shielding their heads with their arms, planned to report their findings, but along what lines we never knew, neither did we care.

There were the usual feuds in the village, between Up End and Down End, Church not speaking to Chapel and even the latter split according to particular sects. There was gossip and scandal as there is in every genuine community with everybody actually revelling in the tales.

Our world was a small one, its boundaries close but, on thinking this over in later years, I have wondered whether this was not a good thing. Our little world was completely sufficient for the needs of most of its inhabitants. A few of the menfolk had been soldiers and were looked upon with some sort of awe since they had been to "foreign parts." The Rector, too, had travelled a great deal in his student days and this led to dark hints by those who were not members of his denomination. My father was looked upon with some suspicion by certain villagers. Did he not go away from home for days on end and sometimes make the train journey to London, returning to buy a round of pints in the *Dog and Duck*?

It was no use Ma telling their wives that Dad had, in one case, been away painting a horse's portrait or that his trip to London was to sell his hunting pictures to Messrs Fores whose shop was then on the corner of Piccadilly and Sackville Street. You could see they "know'd better" by the way they smiled and shook their heads.

London was regarded as a den of iniquity, peopled by pickpockets and pimps. If a man ventured to that place he ought to keep a tight hold on his watch and, as for a woman, well she would be lucky if she wasn't in the family way after a day there, doomed to hang her head in shame for the rest of her life.

No, a trip to Bedford or Northampton was adventure enough for any decent person. You could make the first by getting yourself a lift on Tommy Dodd's carrier van that made the journey there and back once a week, on market day. This would cost you sixpence, just to wet Tommy's whistle, as he said. Getting to Northampton was more complicated and far more expensive, unless you were lucky enough to be able to cadge a lift off a farmer who happened to be driving there. Otherwise, it meant taking yourself to Newport Pagnell and catching a train. Nor was that all. You had to change trains and this was quite an undertaking for a body with all her shopping.

In my story, I may have been a little unkind about the village school, but this I attended for only a short time before going on to the bigger establishment at the nearby town of Newport Pagnell. That village school would have been condemned as primitive and unsanitary by modern standards and I can't think what the educationists of today would have said about the teaching methods.

Sometimes now I get letters from ex-pupils many of whom finished their schooling at the age of twelve or thirteen. The grammar and spelling are good and the descriptive style far better than that of many who remained at more exalted establishments for far longer in later years.

Those were the days when daily life depended largely upon the horse. The horsekeeper was one of the most respected men on any farm and a case of sickness or lameness in one of his charges was regarded almost in the light of a national disaster. We village boys knew nearly every farm horse by name, Captain, Nobby, Trooper and the rest, as well as which ones kicked and which jibbed at their hills.

Ponds gleamed with the white flowers of water crowsfoot and duckweed amongst which orange-bellied newts came to the surface for air. Those aquatic insects, waterboatmen, sculled erratic courses while dragonfly larvae quit their fragile skins.

Not far from the village, the Great Ouse flowed lazily between meadows on which cattle grazed and chewed the cud. Here a boy could enjoy the electrifying feel of cold water on his body. Or he could try to catch roach, dace, or one of those big perch with spiky fins. On sunny days, the huge pike—jack, we called them—would bask on the sparkling surface.

If he felt like doing neither of these things, then a boy could just lie on the bank in the shade of some willow or alder, his nostrils filled with the scents of meadowsweet and catmint. He could watch a moorhen bobbing her tail and listen to her as she clucked to her brood of tiny black chicks. If he remained very still, a heron might drop silently into the shallows, fold its wings by its side and there wait for an unwary fish.

In those days, all the trees were indeed green.

CHAPTER TWO

AT IT AGAIN

MA WAS A great one for brewing. She made wine from dandelions and cowslips, from elderberries, parsnips and rhubarb; I really believe that had it been possible to make old socks ferment she would have produced wine from them too.

I liked the parsnip and rhubarb brewing best. Not because of the flavour of the wine; I was too young to make much distinction about that. But parsnips or rhubarb had to go through the big, iron-framed mangle with the wooden rollers and I was allowed to turn the handle.

This time, though, it was cowslips. The flowers had been gathered, a golden crop, on dewy Spring days by Lizzie who had little gold rings in her ears and a wart with three long hairs on the end of her nose. Sometimes I went to stay with Lizzie and her parents at their Hardmead cottage, away across fields smelling of wild thyme.

The cowslip flowers had been dried in the sun and now they were in the big copper, together with roots of ginger and all sorts of other things, bubbling away while the steam poured out in clouds from under the thick wooden lid and drifted up to the rafters of the big barn. Neighbours, working in their gardens or leaning against doorposts and seeing the steam issuing from the cobwebbed window and from out of the roof where the tiles were missing, would tell each other that "Them Lloyds were at it again."

A visitor from London once said, patronisingly to Ma, "Oh, Mrs Lloyd, what a beautiful copper you have!" and Ma snapped back "Yes, and it's had more wine than washing in it!"

After the boiling, the wine would go into a huge earthenware panchion to stand and ferment with yeast on rafts of toast. While the fragrant fluid was 'working,' the lid from the copper was always put on the panchion for the benefit of the cat who liked to curl up over the warmth and purr himself to sleep.

There was always a cat about and a batch of game bantams. My father's excuse for keeping the bantams, whose eggs were no bigger than those of pigeons, was that they steadied his beagles from rioting on 'feather,' but I think the real reason was that he, a big man himself, was very fond of small creatures.

The bantam cock was as arrogant as any other of his kind, but he was not nearly as fierce as his wives when one of them happened to have a brood of chicks. After having lived on the same premises as those bantams, there was never any need to worry about the beagles if they found themselves among a farmer's poultry: they slunk past.

Kit, a big, old, tabby neuter, did not interfere with the bantams and they left him alone; a mutual respect existed between them, but the cat had trouble now and then from beagle pups when they were still at the nibble-and-pull stage. He would put them in their places with well-placed smacks on the nose, but his claws were seldom out. On the copper lid, when it was placed on top of the fermenting wine, he felt safe, but the practice of jumping up on to it was habit forming.

On the day of the cowslip brewing, for some reason or another, Ma did not cover the panchion. Fortunately, the wine had cooled quite a lot when Kit made his customary leap. I let out a yell of horror. "Ma, the cat's in the wine!"

We had to bath him to get rid of the stickiness. Once before, bathing had been necessary, after he had chased a rat into the privy, and then it took all three of us, with Lizzie acting as watercarrier, to accomplish the task. This time, though, he was almost amenable and submitted to the soaping and swilling in the big tin washtray with no more complaint than an occasional feline growl.

As my father rubbed Kit dry with an old towel kept specially for the animals, a grin creased his wide, rising-sun of a face and he said "I do believe the old beggar's tight!"

When the wine was strained into bottles and jars, there were cat's hairs amongst the ullage and Ma said we were lucky that was all.

This bottle and jar procedure meant that these receptacles had first to be found in sufficient numbers. So many of them had held other liquids since they were emptied of the last brew. There was always a search while the wine was working. Peculiar smelling fluids whose origin was long forgotten were emptied out as cobwebbed bottles and dusty earthenware jars were dug out of cupboards and outbuildings.

Kit had been washed and dried and was sleeping more heavily than usual on that well-marked article of furniture known as the Best Chair, the same one on which Baggage, the beagle bitch, had produced so many litters of pups. A row of bottles and jars waited to receive the wine when it was ready.

"Think we've got enough, Missis?" my father wanted to know. "Yes," Ma replied, "but I've just remembered that I noticed a jar in the dining room cupboard when I was looking for cardboard sheets for Jack to make himself a suit of armour." She had a neat little figure and an impish sense of humour that had earned her the name of "Lady Tintacks" amongst the villagers.

Dad was off like a slipped, if overweight, longdog and he was quickly back with the jar. Anybody could see by the way he carried it that it was full. Sitting on a kitchen chair and gripping the jar between his knees, he struggled with a cork made almost airtight by a scrap of greaseproof paper that stuck up like frilling round a ham.

He sniffed noisily, looked up at Ma, gave a throaty chuckle and said "Elderberry! So *that's* where you hid the last jar!"

"Well, it's time we kept some until it was really mature." Ma snapped back and Dad said that living with her was like having a monkey about, but he caught her a resounding slap on the bottom when he said it.

There were two pubs in that small village. *The Dog and Duck* in Up End and *The Cobley Arms* in Down End. There was none in Calves End and the villagers said this was because the folk who lived there thought themselves above the weaknesses of the flesh. At *The Dog and Duck* in Up End, which was where we lived, Mrs Pawsey, who owned it, brewed her own beer, and good stuff it was, or so I heard those old enough to judge of such matters say.

On most evenings, my father would lay down his palette and brushes and descend the outside ladder that was the only way to his studio, a room that had been a loft before we came to live there. Then, clapping on a tweed hat as protection for his nearly bald head, he would call out to Ma that he was going for a yarn and a pint of Mrs Pawsey's ale.

Dad must have fallen to boasting of Ma's wine-making prowess on the evening of the day when he found the hidden jar of old elderberry wine. By closing time, he had invited a few of the other customers back with him to sample the wine and give their opinions on it.

I was in bed awake with my casement window open, listening to the swifts as they screamed past in swooping flocks or arrived like spent bullets at their nests under the thatch eaves. The late and rosy Spring twilight had brought out the bats when Dad and his friends arrived.

There was Farmer Bugbrooke from the next house; we boys called him Pharaoh behind his back because of his bushy, black beard and his autocratic way with his family and his men. Ernie Spraggins, the cobby little horsedealer, was there too. I recognised his laughter just as I knew the deep voice of Pharaoh. Then I heard the slightly self-conscious speech of Harry, who would come round on his bicycle if some boy or girl hadn't been to school. "The Intendance Man" they called him, and Dad said he always knew when Harry had drunk too much because he began addressing him as "my dear sir," and that he was doing now.

Harry had his dog with him, a big, yellow mongrel named Jack like myself. I heard him being ordered to "Sit!" When my father said the night was far too good to be wasted sitting indoors, I heard the planks of the seat by the front door creak as someone sat down. Dad had built the seat himself and it had a little wooden roof as shelter, right underneath my bedroom window.

I heard Dad booming through the house "Missis, I've brought some fellows to sample that elderberry. Will you bring a drop out, please?"

A few minutes later, hearing the clink of glasses, I could no longer be content with listening; I must see as well as hear. Out of bed I slipped and sat on the seat formed where the window was let into the wide, cavity stonewall of this sixteenth century building.

Ma had handed each of the men a wineglass and was now filling them from a big, white, china jug. Pharaoh wiped his black whiskers after the third swallow had emptied his glass.

"It does you credit, Missis!" he declared.

"Good stuff," said Ernie the horsedealer, politely, careful not to finish his glass right away.

Harry the Intendance sipped at his wine, smacked his lips, murmured "H'mm, not bad, not bad at all! My compliments Mrs Lloyd." He took another sip and made a little bow to Ma, and, at the same time gave a sly kick to Jack the dog, just to remind him to stay under the seat.

Pharaoh muttered into his beard that the glasses were a bit on the small side and Ernie was beginning to giggle. Harry smacked his lips again and said "Ha!" several times. There was not enough light for me to see Ma's face, but I imagined the mischievous expression on it as she collected the empty wine glasses and took them into the house saying that her wine was worthy of bigger ones.

Ma came out again with tumblers and a topped-up jug. Pharaoh said that was better and Ernie stopped giggling to mention that there was nothing like a drop of old elderberry to cure a cold in the head.

Pharaoh agreed and added "You want to put some in a saucepan and hot it up on the hob."

"And with a morsel of ginger in it," said Ernie, giggling again.

"Don't forget the nutmeg and spice," Ma said.

"My dear sir—and, forgive, me, I should say and madam," Harry was slurring his words, "a drop, I say, a tiny drop of rum when the—the–wine is w-warm enough, will cure any c-cold."

Dad's laugh came from somewhere in the internal regions and he said "*Cure a cold*? Blow your bloody head off, I would think!"

Already, Pharaoh was holding out an empty tumbler. Ernie was giggling into the bottom of his and Harry was droning "My dear sir—my dear—sir, this really is the most—most del-delectable stuff!"

"If these glasses aren't big enough, I'll fetch one that is." my father told them and going into the house, came out with a tall celery glass. He filled it with the dark wine to the top of the pattern cut into its graceful side. "There!" said he, triumphantly, "Pass this one round!"

"A loving—loving c-cup!" exclaimed Harry the Intendance "My dear sir, what a grace-gracious jeshture!" Every time he spoke, Jack the dog poked a yellow face out from under the wooden seat.

Our beagles, in what we grandly termed the Kennels, in the back-yard, were joining in the gaiety by raising their voices in that singing which only a pack of hounds can produce.

The tall glass had circulated until it was quite empty and Ma told them "I'm afraid that's the lot! And the next brew won't be drinkable for twelve weeks at least."

Sadly Pharaoh set down the celery glass on the stone flags of the path and Kit, the cat, chose that moment to spring off the roof of Pharaoh's stables which backed onto our garden.

Jack the dog did not like cats and he came out from under the seat like a bolted fox. But Kit feared no dog and leapt on to the dog's back, sticking in all his claws. Pharaoh swore, and taking up his ash stick, struck out with it. Ernie giggled more than before and Harry said "My dear sir, I would—wouldn't have this happen for all the—" I never heard what he wouldn't have it happen for.

My father was swearing too, I gathered because that tinkling sound had marked the end of the antique celery glass and Ma had gone for a dustpan and brush to pick up the remains before some animal trod on it, or I did myself next morning.

Kit stayed on the dog's back just long enough to show him who was boss and then jumped off to stand, tail and fur on end, and watch the dog streak off down the path and clear the gate like a steeple-chaser.

Them Lloyds were at it again.

CHAPTER THREE

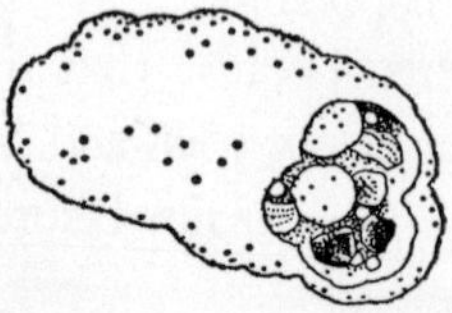

SCHOOL

SLINGING MY SATCHEL over one shoulder, I ran down the garden path as I heard the gate-latch of the cottage opposite. Eric Thorne greeted me "Wotcher!" His mother, wearing a sacking apron and with her hair in curlers, called from the back door "You've got a clanger for your lunch, our Eric, and if you don't eat it, then bring it back!" She gave a half-hearted wave of the hand.

Eric looked up at the low, grey clouds and whistled.

"*Do you hear me, our Eric?*" her voice was shrill now. "If you don't eat the clanger you are to bring it home again!"

"Ah" said Eric, jerking his head and continuing his whistling.

"Don't you like clangers?" I asked, as we walked through Up End.

"They're all right," Eric said "but our Mum will keep on about hers. Seems to think they're marvellous even after they've been hotted up two or three times on the school stove."

Two counties in England each claim the clanger as a native dish. Bedfordshire knows it as a Bedfordshire Clanger, while Bucks calls it a Buckinghamshire Clanger, and Washbrook is just on the Bucks side of the border.

The clanger was thought up as the perfect meal for the farm labourer to take out into the fields, to be eaten when he heard the One O'clock Bell being rung in the church tower, telling him it was 'bavor time.' A clanger had a casing of suet pastry through which the eater gnawed his way with happy anticipation, knowing that if he had chosen the right end, he would soon taste meat, onions and potatoes.

Working his strong jaws, he would eat on, perhaps sitting comfortably with his feet in a ditch and a sack over his head and shoulders until in time he reached the jam at the other end. He had a right to enjoy it when the meat was from his own pig, the onions and potatoes grown by himself and the casing made, and the whole thing cooked, by the woman he had married. The ability to make a good clanger was an important asset to the girl who was looking for a husband.

Eric and I walked down the gentle hill beside which rippled the little brook that not only added to the beauty of the village but also helped the simple sanitation of a small dwelling called Honeymoon Cottage. As we came to that part of the village known as Down End and the patch of grass, the Knoll, with its iron pump, we were joined by Waggle who, after we had exchanged "wotchers" asked what Eric had brought for his lunch.

"A clanger," said Eric "what you got?"

"Cold bacon, with plenty of fat."

Nobody asked about my lunch, for I had grandparents in Newport Pagnell who gave me a hot meal on schooldays. There was a school, too, in our village, presided over by a red-headed whippet of a man whom we boys knew as Little Arriwig because we likened him to an earwig. After some argument with the school authorities which we did not understand, the parents of some of us had transferred their sons to the bigger school in the market town of Newport. This meant a walk of two miles at each end of the day, but that only added to our chances of fun.

Ahead of us we could see another group of boys walking in the same direction. "It's them big 'uns," Waggle said. "Don't let's catch up with them. You know what Lanky is like." Lanky was the bully of the party and most of us had felt his fists at some time or another.

A sound that might have been made by some gigantic bumblebee in distress grew in volume; there was a honking as of a rather hoarse gander and a big, open, touring car rounded the bend we had just passed.

"Here comes Old Billy!" cried Eric, and we all three started dancing up and down in the middle of the road and yelling "Give us a ride, mister!"

Old Billy was the disrespectful name by which we knew William Cobley, Colonel of Yeomanry, Justice of the Peace and a dedicated foxhunter. Seeing our antics, he brought his car to a stop in a cloud of dust. We touched our caps and said "Good morning, sir."

"Get in boys. Be careful of the paintwork and if you don't sit still and keep quiet, I'll make you get out and walk again."

"Yes, sir" we chorused, as Old Billy performed some rite that set the vehicle in motion again. We were off, perched proudly on the leather seat of a real motor car.

As we bowled along past the Big 'uns, Eric thumbed his nose at them and Waggle stuck out a long, pink tongue. We draped ourselves over the back of the car to watch the results.

The Big 'uns were scowling and shaking their fists. Petty picked up a stone and threw it but his aim was bad. We howled with laughter and Eric stood up in the back of the car and did a war dance until he fell down. I took off Waggle's cap and waved it.

Old Billy barked "How can I concentrate on driving when you boys are behaving like little monkeys?"

"Yes, sir," and we sat down again, smirking.

Our ride brought us into Newport at an unusually early hour and we had time to watch the sheep and cattle being driven into the pens set up on the Market Square. The air was full of bleating and lowing, of the smell of cowdung and the cloying scent of wool; drovers were shouting *how-how-how*! and rattling their sticks on hurdles, when they were not thwacking them on the quarters of some poor beast that was not hurrying to what might well be its last penning.

Waggle said, "When we are going home this evening, I'll bet them big 'uns set about us."

"Best thing we can do," I suggested, "is to cadge another ride before they catch us."

"What if nobody will give us one?" Eric wanted to know.

"Tell you what," said Waggle brightly, "if they *do* go for us, it will be that 'orrible Lanky and you and I could fix him between us, Jack."

"How?" I ventured to ask, not feeling very keen on the idea.

"Easy," replied Waggle, "I'll hold him round the waist and kick his shins while you punch him in the face. I'll do the kicking 'cos I got boots and you only wear shoes."

Eric shook his head. "Two on to one ain't fair." he declared.

"It's fair enough when he's bigger than you," Waggle said.

The school bell was ringing with that urgent note of all school bells and we ran through the High Street, satchels slapping on our hips as we dodged the market floats and gigs and laughed at the angry shouts of their drivers.

School was not so bad if you didn't think about it too much and if the teacher didn't pick on you. The mornings wore on in an atmosphere of chalk dust and unwashed clothes, with a break in the middle when we all rushed out to release our pent-up energy in shouts, pushes and punches as we scampered on the asphalt playground now steaming as the sun grew stronger.

The second half of the morning passed even more quickly than the first and I ran off to my grandparents' home, The Firs, that stood back in a big, walled garden. This was where, last year, I had disgraced myself by imagining the freshly placed beansticks to be Red Indians and neatly decapitating each one with my shilling tomahawk. Grandpa, an enthusiastic gardener, had plucked his whiskers and exclaimed "Drat the boy!" the nearest this good man who sang bass in chapel, ever came to swearing.

My dinner was late on this day, for Grandma had gone to Northampton to do her weekly shopping and Grandpa, after a walk round the cattle market, had made the most of the opportunity to visit the Red Lion and take a glass or so of Irish whiskey of which he was very fond.

As a result, I went into class breathless on the last clang of the afternoon bell and, later, got a rap on the knuckles with the cane for not paying attention to what the teacher was saying.

School over for the day, we younger boys hurried off as quickly as we could, hoping our departure had not been seen by the Big 'uns. We walked and ran through the town, and over the North Bridges where there were recesses built for people to take refuge from passing stage coaches, or so we had been told. But we could hear the clump of hobnailed boots behind and we knew that the Big 'Uns were after us.

"If only someone would come by and give us a lift!" said Waggle, looking back over his shoulder. Eric, whose senses were as sharp as a stoat's, said he could hear Ezra Peabody's shandrydan coming out of town. "Know the sound of his old pony's hooves a mile away."

"He won't take three of us," Waggle said gloomily.

Eric, always with his wits about him, said the thing to do was for two of us to hide behind the hedge whilst the third begged a lift. Then, if he got it, while Ezra was driving off the others could run out and jump on the back axle.

We didn't think much of the suggestion, but almost anything would be better than being overtaken by the Big 'Uns, whose shouts and tread we could hear behind us. Waggle and I clambered over a stile and crouched behind the hawthorn hedge, all fresh and green with young leaf. Peering through the twigs, we could see Eric standing at the roadside, holding one foot and pretending to sob.

Cloppity-clop, along came the fat pony that must have been nearly as old as the crusty old chap who sat in the ramshackle cart to which it was harnessed.

"Muster Peabody," Eric wailed, sobbing more loudly than before, "Oh, Muster Peabody—".

"Out of my way, boy!" shouted the old man in a cracked voice, standing up and flourishing his whip. "Out of my way, you know this pony is a hot 'un!"

Waggle and I were disgusted with such unfeeling behaviour and, climbing back over the stile, we shuffled our feet on the road and made rude noises between pursed lips. This set the pony as near alight as it was ever likely to be again and, after breaking wind three times, it actually shook itself into a shambling gallop.

Ezra Peabody fell back on to the seat. He brandished his whip at us, the ricketty cart creaked threateningly and he piped "Whoa, whoa! Devil fetch the boys, you know this pony bolts! *Whoa, whoa!* I'll report you to Long Bob, all three of you. Yes, I know who you are. *Whoa, whoa!*"

Long Bob was the village constable and besides being Lanky's father, he wore a wide leather belt around his waist and was uncommonly quick to take it off and use it on boys who made a nuisance of themselves. And he never smiled. The Big 'Uns were coming nearer. When we looked round we could see the heads of Lanky and Petty showing over the hedge beyond the bend in the road. They were shouting and laughing. "There's three of them," said Waggle "Dodger's not tall enough to see over the hedge—but he's strong as an ox. Our dad says so."

"Kipper is sure to be with them and he makes four," I said. Kipper was Lanky's brother, a shrimp of a boy cowed by his father's belt and his brother's fists.

"He don't count," Eric said "If there's a fight, he'll bawl his eyes out and run home to tell Long Bob."

The Big 'Uns had rounded the corner. Lanky and Petty were striding out and the other two trotting to keep up with them. They were passed by a stout cob drawing a pig float with a jolly, round-faced man driving and singing as he drove. His feet dangled over the front of the float and he was Mr Ridley from Hilbury. It was clear to any country boy that he was market merry.

"Allo, Muster Ridley" we chorused, hopefully running into the middle of the road. "Have you had a good market?"

"Yes, I have. Trade was very good, very good indeed. And now I suppose you young beggars want a lift for your cheek. Ah, well, jump up!"

Mr Ridley said "whoa there!" and pulled the cob to a stop, an action that jerked his greenish bowler hat over his eyes. We scrambled over the high tailboard and found ourselves sitting on top of three large black sows that were prevented from jumping out by the net that covered tham.

Pushing his hat back into its proper position, Mr Ridley shook the reins and clicked his tongue. The sows squealed and we boys shouted "Yah!" at the Big 'Uns who were shaking their fists. The cob, its coat shiny with health, grooming and good grazing, stepped out at a sharp trot and Mr Ridley, after twirling the lash round the whipstock with the skill of a professional coachman, began to sing.

"There he was with his wooden leg up, like a shovel
stuck up in a cartload o' muck,
Singing diddledum-daree,
Fly away Mary . . ."

But something was happening to the float. Its front was rising higher and its tail dropping lower. Eric, very white in the face, was sliding over the tailboard and on to the hard road with its granite chippings.

CHAPTER FOUR

SKY HIGH

WE WERE A squirming heap on the road, two boys, Mr Ridley who was swearing quietly to himself chiefly because he had lost his bowler hat, and the three sows who were squealing and kicking with their legs through the net. The pig-float rested on its tailboard, shafts sticking up in the air like the wooden leg in Mr Ridley's song. The cob was standing quietly as if this sort of thing happened every day.

On the grass verge, Eric thoughtfully felt a bulge in his satchel to make sure the clanger was intact. "I knew the breeching was going," he said, meaning part of the harness.

"Then why the devil didn't you say so, you stupid little bleeder?" demanded Mr Ridley as he retrieved his hat from under a sow's belly and pushed a dent out of its crown. "Now help me with these damned pigs. Here, let's get the float upright first and I'll mend the breeching with a bit of bagstring."

It was no simple task but, between us, we dealt with it while we three boys pretended to ignore the presence of the Big 'Uns who had caught up and now stood, hands in pockets, grinning like Chinese masks at our struggles. At last, the damage was repaired to Mr Ridley's satisfaction and he climbed on to the front of the float again.

"No, you ain't going to ride again. Caused enough trouble as it is, you have. Gee-up there, Joey!" and off he drove, the cob's hooves clip-clopping and Mr Ridley singing away about the wooden leg without a thought for us and the fact that we now had to face the Big 'Uns.

We started walking. Eric was whistling *The Minstrel Boy* but, whichever way we headed, there was either Petty or Lanky in our path. Waggle set his small jaw and gave Lanky a push.

"All right!" Lanky said "You started this." He punched Waggle in the chest. Like a game terrier at a bigger dog, Waggle sprang and, grabbing Lanky round the waist, started kicking him on the shins.

Waggle and I had gone over the whole operation in words so many times during the day that I knew exactly what to do, and I rained punch after punch on Lanky's face. I had to reach up above my own head to do it, but had the satisfaction of seeing blood come streaming from his nose.

Kipper scuttled off down the road, rubbing the tears from his cheeks and burbling something about "telling our dad." Petty and Dodger were walking in the same direction, saying loudly that they never started it. When at last Waggle released his clutch on Lanky and I stopped punching, the tall boy followed the other Big 'Uns in silence, sometimes stopping to pluck handfuls of grass from the roadside with which to staunch his bleeding.

News of the battle had gone before us by means of one of those mysterious methods of communication which, in an English village, are the equal of jungle drums. A few of the very young children had composed a jingle which they chanted as they ran to meet us.

"Waggle, Waggle, on the run,
Kicked old Lanky on the bum."

But they stopped as we neared the Knoll. Two girls were standing there and, obviously, such a coarse expression must not be used in front of them. Nancy's wits were as sharp as her features and she was about a year and a half older than her brother Eric. Waggle's sister was two years older than Waggle and had all the promise of growing into a blonde beauty. Both went to the village school and Effie was sometimes put in charge of the youngest children. Waggle and I felt uncomfortably guilty under the disapproving gaze of Effie.

Effie ran her blue eyes over us, and almost unconsciously I pulled the wrinkles out of my stockings while Eric pursed his lips and started on the first bars of *The Minstrel Boy*. Being her brother, Waggle pretended indifference.

"*I* know what they are saying about our Waggle." Effie said and Eric stopped whistling. "They say 'Waggle, Waggle on the run, kicked old Lanky'—" we held our breaths as she hesitated and then her final words came out with a rush. "Kicked old Lanky, I'll tell our mum!"

In the tow of his sister, Waggle went off towards their house which stood near the Knoll and the others of the party walked past Honeymoon Cottage that was built of wattle and daub and had a thatched roof over its two rooms. There was a wooden shack behind Honeymoon Cottage and within this was a plank with two round holes, one large and the other small, spanning the narrow stream. So this ancient cottage could claim to owning the only water closet in the village.

Honeymoon Cottage was reserved for newly married couples who, as soon as the union looked like proving fruitful, were expected to move to more commodious quarters and so leave the field clear for the next couple. It is possible that men who fought at Crecy and others who carried billhooks in the Peasants' Revolt were conceived in Honeymoon Cottage.

We were opposite the cottage when Nancy Thorne stopped and said "Coo, have you heard about Aggie Lute? Just passing here she was when it happened"

"What happened?" Eric and I wanted to know and then we were told the full story. Aggie Lute was a spinster, rather past the mark o 'mouth, as Ernie Spraggins the horsedealer put it. It seemed that she was hustling her gaunt body through the village after doing a bit of scrubbing for Mrs Cobley at the Grange when she found herself abreast of Honeymoon Cottage. There, no doubt—though this idea did not enter our young heads—what little imagination she had took charge and she began to daydream, he mouth falling open and showing her uneven, rather big teeth,

Nancy went on with her story. "Chuck Turney was driving a cow to Pharaoh Bugbrooke's bull and when it saw poor Aggie, it took one look, lowered its head and went straight at her—*just like that*!" Nancy made a thrusting gesture with her right arm. I waited expectantly but Eric feigned boredom at his sister's graphic demonstration.

"And what then?" I asked.

Nancy pursed her lips and wrinkled her young brow in a frown. "Tossed her, it did. Tossed her *sky high*!" she declared dramatically.

"Cor, *is she dead*?" I asked with all the relish of the ghoul that is dormant in most young children.

"No, not dead. But we thought she was never coming down again and now that she has, she's got the virgin's ammonia!"

Impressed with this bit of information, we walked in silence for some minutes until I piped up "What is a virgin?"

"*You* know," said Nancy, "you only find them in the Bible."

"Don't be silly!" Eric snorted. "It's just like a heifer what's never been bulled. And that's more than you can say about Totsie Varley down Blackthorn Lane."

"Now then, our Eric!" Nancy snapped "If you say that sort of thing again I'll tell our mum!" I was impressed that while Kipper ran to tell "our dad," it was "our mum" who was the threat in the Thorne family. Nancy changed the subject. "Did you eat your clanger, our Eric?"

"No, it was a bit hard like," Eric fingered the bulge in his satchel and stared at his feet. Then he brightened and added "but it broke my fall when the breeching on Mr Ridley's pig-float bust and it tipped us all out, arse over head!"

It did not occur to me to be surprised that while the harmless euphemism in the jingle was taboo, a four letter Anglo-Saxon vulgarity was permissible.

We were home now and brother and sister went clattering up their garden path, a pleasing mosaic of broken earthenware. As I opened our own gate I heard the throaty chorus of the beagles in the backyard and was soon being greeted by the merry imps, their tongues licking my bare knees, their claws tugging at my stockings. Smelling tea, I hurried in through the back door.

"A bit late, aren't you, boy?" my father grinned and set down his big cup.

"Yes, what have you been up to this time?" Ma wanted to know.

"O-oh!" I cried, revelling in the suspense, "What *do* you think? We cadged a ride on Mr Ridley's pig-float and the breeching broke and the cart tipped up and threw us all on the road."

As I paused for breath, Ma asked "Have you heard about poor Miss Lute?"

"What, Aggie?" I burst in, breath now recovered. "Yes, she was tossed by a cow, sky high, Nancy Thorne says, and now she's got the virgin's ammonia!"

"The *what*, boy?" Dad spluttered over his tea.

"The virgin's ammonia," I repeated, slowly and, I hoped, impressively "Nancy says so."

Ma got to her feet and said she was going to see Nancy's mother, opposite, and find out about this unique complaint.

I was finishing my tea when Ma came back. "Well, Missis, let's hear the truth!" Dad said.

"The fact is," Ma told us, "poor Aggie Lute had delayed shock and now she is on the verges of pneumonia, or so the village nurse says."

The kitchen window was open to let in the sweet Spring air as well as the fragrance of Pharaoh Bugbrooke's muckyard which was on the other side of the garden wall. Flocks of swifts were swooping and screaming after the swarms of small flies and the old cat was purring away like a kettle on the windowsill.

There came another sound, the clatter of feet and the high-pitched voice of Mrs Thorne shouting "Stop her, stop her! She's got our Eric's clanger!"

All three of us ran out into the strip of garden and were in time to meet Baggage, the best brood bitch of all my father's beagles. I must have left the garden gate open, for Baggage was heading for our back door. Between her jaws was the Bucks clanger that Eric had carried to school and back.

The boy himself was standing, hands in pockets, and I heard the very faint strains of *The Minstrel Boy* being whistled. Behind his mother's back, he was, no doubt, congratulating himself upon having seen the last of that delicacy.

CHAPTER FIVE

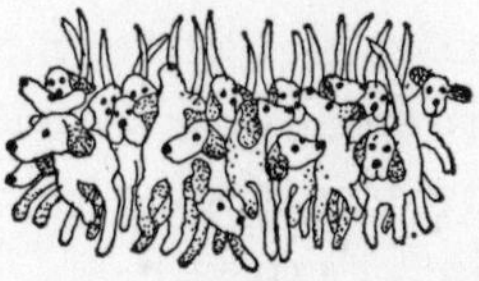

TOTSIE

IT WAS SATURDAY, which meant no school and, instead, that extraordinary procedure my father called "morning exercise."

Dewdrops sparkled on isolated patches of grass between holes scratched by the beagles and bantams on what we grandly termed "the lawn." Two sparrows flew up, chirping, and perched on the guttering of Pharaoh's stone-built stables and, in the yard between the back door and the kennels, Kit, the big tabby, crouched, slit-eyed and with a twitching tail as he stared unblinkingly at a blackbird chattering defiance from a branch of the elder bush.

The blackbird ceased his chatter and watched, head on one side, as my father, tweed hat cocked over horn-rimmed spectacles on a nose flattened by a long-forgotten rugger game, walked to the garden gate and opened it. I stood by the kennel door.

The beagles, recognising all the symptoms, were baying and singing and yelping in anticipation. "Let 'em out boy!" bellowed Dad.

I lifted the latch and the door was forced open by the rush of small black, tan and white bodies. Through the yard they poured, while Kit sprang effortlessly on to the narrow rim of a water butt. They rushed down the garden path and Ma, putting her head out of the dining-room window, cried "Tally-ho, gone away!"

My father, big though he was, staggered slightly as the wave of hounds flowed so forcefully around and past him.

Tow-wow, tow-wow! they chorused, their scampering pads raising puffs of dust from the dry village street. Cats fled, tails and fur bristling, other dogs tucked in their own tails and scuttled into backyards then turned and barked fiercely. Even our own pugnacious bantam cock, who had been taking a dust bath in the middle of the road, flapped his wings, crowed and led his cackling harem to a safe perch on the thatched roof of Sal Heffer's cottage.

From all along the street came sounds of slamming doors and a shrill female voice declaring that she'd report them Lloyds to Long Bob and have the law on them. One front door was not shut quickly enough and into the house slipped a handsome tricolour doghound appropriately named Poacher. The housewife was so interested in what was happening outside that she did not notice. Neither did she spot him as he came out of the back door carrying a pork chop between his jaws.

Tow-wow, tow-wow! The beagles continued on their wild career. Dad leaned on a gatepost and lit a Woodbine. "Get round 'em, boy!" he roared. "Get round 'em, instead of standing there grinning like an idiot!" He wiped his glasses with a red spotted handkerchief, then mopped his brow and I raced after the last beagle while trying to crack a small whip and piping "Steady there!" and "Gerraway back!" as I had heard that foxhound whipper-in rating a stray hound.

After a time, the "first fine, careless rapture" wore off and most of the beagles waited for me, sterns slowly waving, tongues lolling out and expressions of innocence on their faces. I muttered terrible threats and Melody, who was one of the most mischievous, rolled on her back and wriggled.

Dad came round the corner past the lamp post to which was fixed a letter box that had been the target for so many catapults. No boy of the village was thought worthy of notice by the Big 'Uns until he had shattered the enamel collection plate and got away with it uncaught by Long Bob.

"Have you counted them, boy?" Dad wanted to know "*Then*

why not? Count them now. Oh, and take that chop away from Poacher. Drop it over the hedge—or, better still, wrap your handkerchief round the thing and put it in your pocket."

I tried to count the beagles as we moved on, but they were like so much quicksilver and I had to keep starting over again. "Well?" said my father "Are they all on?"

"I—I'm not sure, Dad." Desperately I looked over the pied bodies. "Old Baggage is missing," I said.

"She always is by the time we get here. Slip back and see if you can find her, and when you do, give her one to go on with."

I ran off back along the street while Dad clicked his tongue, tucked his whip under one arm, lit another Woodbine and led the rest of the pack in the direction of Calves End, that section of the village noted for its respectability. There was no pub in Calves End and Long Bob, the policeman, lived there; there was an austere chapel, and no goings-on, or if there were, few knew about them, and they never talked.

I dropped to a walk, going the way I had come, whistling and calling Baggage's name as I crossed the little bridge which many villagers did not know was there. We boys were aware of it though, spanning as it did a ditch that was in the habit of running dry about the time the parson's apples were ripe. And the ditch was a means of reaching his orchard, if you wriggled under the bridge on your belly. Now, red and white sprays of apple blossom buds were peeking up over the wall, along the top of which broken glass had been cemented to stop the inroads of thieving boys.

At the corner of Blackthorn Lane I stopped to look and listen, but I saw no signs of Baggage's passing, no panic, no flutterings nor other commotions; nor did I hear any execrations or banging of doors. Not that there were many doors to slam in Blackthorn Lane, but just a starkly plain row of three yellow brick cottages with, beyond them and standing alone, *The Lilacs*, a white stone building rather too big to be a cottage but not quite big enough to be a house.

Perhaps the missing beagle was in Blackthorn Lane, and I walked along its rough and narrow length to find out. She might even have gone beyond the end and now be hunting Pharaoh Bugbrooke's rabbits, though in that case I was sure to have heard Baggage, for she was, as my father said, a trifle free with her tongue.

A blackbird was fluting away among white plum blossom in the carefully tended garden of the cottage and, somewhere in the rear, a sow grunted contentedly. I had a mental picture of a litter of pink piglets nuzzling into the heaving flank. I could smell the pigs too and their scent mixed with that of soapsuds in the roadside ditch and a faint whiff from the small sheds set at a few yards distance from the back doors.

Few people went down Blackthorn Lane other than those who lived there and the postman, and Fred Fowler once a week to collect the rent. At least, few were *seen* to go down there, though the women of the village whispered to each other behind raised hands and with much jerking of chins, that plenty did go and that they were all men and went after dark.

The Varleys lived at *The Lilacs*, Ned, Dolly his wife and their daughter Totsie. Ned, a colourless, insignificant scrap of a man did 'odd jobs' in the district, though not often enough to interfere with his hobby which was the consumption of beer. Yet, such news items being known to all in a village, it was said that the Varleys contrived to live very well indeed. There was no cutting down to bread and dripping for dinner when the second side of bacon had diminished and the next pig was not ready for killing. Even while such a hiatus lasted the Varleys were able to eat meat.

Other women who lived in the village marvelled at the amount plump and jolly Dolly Varley spent at Mrs Perry's shop where, when you had got over the first shock of the loudly clanging door-bell, you were confronted with everything a housewife might need. On one counter were the groceries, on another joints of meat (Mrs Perry's son Ted did the butchering) and, on the floor in between an assortment of pots and pans, the oil stoves on which to heat them. So Dolly Varley had plenty of scope for spending.

Totsie was the source of the Varley affluence. She was what is preciously described as a well-built girl and she had raven hair, an undeniably pretty face with pink cheeks and pleasing dimples. There was a mole just above one corner of her full-lipped mouth. When she smiled at a stranger in the *Red Lion* in Newport, he found himself repeating well-worn clichés about innocent village maidens. If he had enough money in his pocket he was quickly disillusioned on both counts.

The village lads were beneath Totsie's notice, for the simple reason that, on a farm labourer's wages they could not afford the price of her favours. So they feigned indifference. "Wouldn't touch her with a bargepole" and so on. But Totsie had a bicycle to take her into Newport where, in the *Red Lion* she lingered over a half-pint of mild beer.

Totsie's best clients were the virile, carefree, young men who came to a nearby vicarage to be crammed for the Services or the universities. These high-spirited youths regarded Totsie as part of the establishment, much as they did the hunters they hired from Ernie Spraggins. After lights out, they climbed out of their bedroom windows, mounted bicycles and pedalled through the darkness to the warm welcome that always awaited them at *The Lilacs*.

Sometimes of an evening in the *Dog and Duck*, Turnips Thorne and Stumper his elder brother would try to draw Ned Varley about the goings on in his house, but their wits were as heavy as the clay soil they so often trod and Ned declined to be drawn. The truth is, he divided his time between the taproom of the *Dog and Duck* and his own garden, especially if Totsie was entertaining visitors. Dolly, his wife, was always ready to open the front door and to brew a pot of tea or even pour a glass of dandelion wine for likely looking visitors.

One night, after a shaft from Stumper had gone home, Ned went back to *The Lilacs* with his head filled with good resolutions and his belly with Mrs Pawsey's strong ale. Finding no visitors there, he thumped the table until the unwashed crockery danced, and announced alcoholically that, from now on, there would be no more goings on in his home. "This has always been a respectable 'ouse, and a respectable 'ouse it's going to stay!" he concluded with an extra heavy thump that cracked a willow pattern milk jug.

Ned had astonished himself with his own vehemence and he paused to enjoy the effect. His enjoyment did not last long. Dolly picked up a saucepan from the kitchen range and slammed it down on Ned's head. "You great fool!" said she "Don't you know where the money comes from?"

Young as I was, I knew there was something different about life at *The Lilacs*. A knowledge of the 'facts of life' comes early to most country children and I had no illusions about the reasons for the visits of that magnificent Shire stallion his mane and tail plaited with gay ribbons, to Pharaoh Bugbrooke's mares, nor about the mating details of our beagles; but I was a little mystified about the goings on at *The Lilacs*. There seemed to be no end product.

I was passing the gate, flanked as it was on either side by the bushes from which the house took its name, when I heard a hound's whimper. Not a whimper of distress nor tinged with excitement, but expressing pleasure. I looked at the house, framed with the fresh young leaves and buds of the lilac bushes. There, at an open window, was Baggage.

The beagle had her forepaws on the window ledge, her long tongue was lolling out and there was a look of voluptuous contentment on her cunning old face. Dolly Varley's plump arm was around her neck, and, on her other side, Totsie was stroking one of her big, silky ears.

"Looking for your doggy?" Dolly giggled. I said that I was.

"Then you can come and fetch her," said Totsie with a smile that entrenched the mole in a dimple. I felt a strange, tingling attraction as I opened the little wooden slatted gate and walked on a path made of broken tiles and bits of china.

Totsie herself held the door open in such a way that I had to duck under her arm when her mother called out "Come in." I was con-

scious of a faint, strangely exciting odour that I knew was not artificial scent, and of a billowing softness aganist my right shoulder.

Dolly Varley was now holding Baggage in her arms like a baby and crooning to her, while that wicked old fraud looked as if she was enjoying every second of it. She even put out her tongue and licked Dolly's cheek.

"Poor thing!" said Dolly "Anyone can see she's hungry by the look in her eyes. Every morning she comes to see us and we always give her a feed."

I could not disillusion them by telling the truth, that Baggage had an appetite that was the equal of two normal dogs and that she had to be fed by herself as, otherwise, she would take the food intended for the rest of the pack after she had wolfed her own share.

As I took the beagle from Dolly Varley, I felt an arm slide across my shoulders and knew again that intriguing odour. Then Totsie bent her head, kissed me on the forehead and said I was a nice little boy.

I ran down the garden path and did not put Baggage down until I was out in the lane again. Still I ran, the old beagle with me, her full tummy swinging. A jumble of new thoughts crowded each other in my mind; but I did wish Totsie hadn't used the word 'little.'

When I came up to my father and the rest of the pack, he was leaning on a field gate and looking on to the paddock known as Oliver's Piece because it was said that the Lord Protector had mounted a canon there to command the Hilbury Heights. Oliver's Piece was common land and any villager had a right to graze his cattle on it, which is why Poor Arry was there. He kept a few head of screw cows and never grazed them on his own bare acres if free grass was to be found elsewhere.

Poor Arry was leaning on a blackthorn stick, his watery eyes staring into the distance and his red nose dripping on to a thin, tobacco-stained moustache.

Dad turned round and took the eternal Woodbine out of his own mouth. "You've been long enough, boy! Anyhow, where did you find the old bitch? Where had she gone to ground?"

"In *The Lilacs*," I told him. "They told me she goes in there every day for a feed."

Dad's face broadened even more as he grinned and said "The greedy old devil! But did you go inside? No wonder your face is red! Were you raped, boy?" This was a new one for me and I made a mental note to ask the schoolmaster the meaning of the simple word.

My father straightened his broad back, stubbed out the fag-end on the gatepost and boomed "What are you standing about for? Got Totsie on your mind? Just look what those hounds are up to! There's Barmaid and little Weasel working the hedgerow after rabbits, though a fat lot of chance they have of finding one when they've all been poached. Haven't they, Arry?"

Poor Arry nodded his head and the action had the effect of sending a shower of spray off his moustache. "Ah, seem'ly!" he said. He always said "seem'ly" when he agreed, meaning, it was thought, "seemingly."

"There are Drama and Dramatist playing silly beggars twenty-one up" my father went on, jerking a thumb in the direction of a couple of black and white hounds who were chasing each other in circles. "Oh, and there go those useless brutes Patrick and Poacher. Remind me to draft them to someone I don't like." He let out a bellow "What are you at, blast your hides, what are you at?" then he turned round to me. "Get round 'em, boy, *get round 'em*!"

Patrick and Poacher, two handsome hounds who were little use in the hunting field, were streaking along the footpath giving tongue on the line of a skinny mongrel that could be viewed as it scuttled uphill in the direction of its owner who was scratching his allotment garden with a broken fork.

"Get round 'em boy!" my father said again, at the same time hurling his tweed hat at black and tan Ruby to stop her from rolling in a cowpat.

CHAPTER SIX

THE WHEELWRIGHT

WHEN, AFTER ABOUT twenty minutes and with much shouting and whip-cracking, I had 'got round' our pack of small beagles, we went on with them through Calves End and round by the pond into Down End, my father giving a cheery wave and greeting to everybody within sight and quite indifferent to whether these drew any response.

Mrs Pyecroft was in the stackyard of Elm Tree Farm, her eyes on a flock of poultry as they scratched and pecked at the rutted ground between the ricks.

"Morning, Mrs Pyecroft," Dad said, taking off his shapeless hat and then tugging it back on his bald head. He leaned on the five-barred gate and gazed critically at the dozen or so crossbred hens and the rather bedraggled Rhode Island cock. "Lay plenty of eggs?" he asked.

"Not bad," replied the farmer's widow, placing capable hands on broad hips. "They lay fairly well, but its not much use setting their eggs. There'd be very few chickens. The old chap is getting a bit beyond it. Reckon I'll have to wring his neck and put him on the table, then get myself a younger one. Ah, well, it comes to them all in time!"

As we moved on, Dad made a cautious comment on the weather, knowing that this was always a ticklish subject with farmers. Mrs

Pyecroft beamed. "Lovely weather, Mr Lloyd!" said she "Lovely weather. Rains all nights and Sundays and don't stop the lads a-muck carting!"

An iron pump enclosed in a wooden casing stuffed with straw as protection against the frosts of winter stood in the middle of a patch of grass known as the Knoll. The handle was being worked by a wisp of a woman whose sacking apron was tucked up around her waist and whose head was crowned with a wide-brimmed, rather dilapidated, straw hat. My father waved, but she paused in her pumping for only long enough to dart him a snakelike glare out of red-rimmed eyes.

Old Jinny was certain in her warped little mind that all men were evil, especially those who frequented taverns, kept dogs and painted pictures. A hundred or so years earlier, the poor old body would have been burned as a witch.

Nobody ever thought of oiling the pump handle and when being worked, it gave out a noise like the braying of a randy jackass. This was part of a morning symphony made up of the slow clip-clop of a horse's hooves as it drew one of Widow Pyecroft's muck carts, the singing of a robin from a tree in front of Mrs Perry's emporium and the ring of hammer on anvil.

The musical *clink-clink*, pause, *clink-clink*, pealed like a bell above it all and I imagined Tom Barnes inside his smithy, the glow on the stone walls lighting or fading as his son, big Bill, who was apprenticed to the trade, worked the massive bellows or stayed his hand. A horseshoe would be glowing as Tom turned it in the grip of the long-handled pincers. I imagined too, the horse munching oats from a nosebag as it stood waiting to be shod.

Evan Hughes was leaning on the lower half of the double door of his wheelwright's shop, sniffing the exhilarating spring air with his thin, rather disapproving nose. When Dad called out "Good morning Mr Hughes," Evan raised a hand and I wondered whether the gesture was meant to ask for a blessing on us or to register a protest. For Evans was one of those people with a mission to set the world to rights—or as much of it as came within the range of his perceptions.

"Think we're going to have a drop of rain?" my father asked, blinking through his spectacles at the scudding clouds.

"We must resign ourselves to accept what the Lord may send us," Evan replied, looking down his nose.

"Alleluiah!" exclaimed Dad, without the flicker of a smile.

"Mock not the ways of the Lord!" proclaimed Evan, shaking his head. "For the blasphemers shall be cast into the outer darkness."

"I know. Where there shall be weeping and wailing and gnashing of teeth." Dad set his feet apart and jammed his hands deep into trouser pockets. He could quote the Bible and William Shakespeare with equal ease. "But I had no intention of blaspheming."

There was a look of disapproval on the wheelwright's face and he was in the middle of something further about loose speech when a varminty-looking, leggy terrier darted out of the side passage of a cottage and, hackles up, began yapping and snarling insults at the beagles.

Until this happened, the little hounds had been standing docilely around my father, sterns waving, great deceptively innocent brown eyes on his every movement. The appearance of the terrier acted like an electric current on them. In a rush of small bodies, they ran at the terrier which immediately spun round and dashed back into the passageway. The beagles, all eight of them, crowded into the narrow space, and that was exactly what the terrier wanted them to do.

Bearing the name of Flash, the terrier belonged to Fred Perry who gave it the sort of life such dogs like, with plenty of ratting and rabbiting. As soon as the hounds were crowded into the alleyway, those in the rear trying to scramble over the backs of those in front, those in front bracing their forelegs to stop them going any further, Flash turned and faced them, lips curled above sharp, snapping teeth.

The joyful baying turned to woeful howling and there was much scrambling to get out faster than they had gone in. Flash got in a nip or two and Poacher came out like a rat from its hole, stern down and tucked between his hindlegs. Only Baggage stood her ground, forefeet apart, tan head lowered. But Flash had no intention of fighting a lady; instead quite the reverse and soon the two were sniffing and prancing around each other.

My father retrieved his hat which he had hurled after the flying pack as they went into their first rush, "Get round 'em, boy, get round 'em!" he bellowed once more and, dusting the hat on his elbow, began swearing eloquently.

"Mr Lloyd, Mr Lloyd!" exclaimed Evan with withering disapproval "The Lord abhors cursing and swearing."

"Then it's very unlikely that he keeps dogs!" replied Dad. "Ah, I see the commotion has brought out Aggie Lute. She must have got over her tossing."

"A righteous woman, Mr Lloyd, a truly righteous—I might almost say saintly—woman, who attends chapel every time the doors are opened. Miss Lute gazes not upon the wine when it is red nor does she lust after the fleshpots of Egypt."

"Why should she look as far as Egypt for her fleshpots? If she shows as much of herself again to Chuck Turney as she did when the cow tossed her, then she won't need to go any further than this village. Really, there's no need to go all that far to find a bit of fun." I saw the mischievous twinkle in Dad's eye and ran to send Baggage back to the pack and, at the same time to hide my blushing, as I heard him say "The boy here called on Totsie Varley this morning."

"Mention not that name in my hearing, Mr Lloyd! Every night I go down on my knees and pray that that woman may be delivered from the fate of Rahab the harlot!" Evan turned back into his shop that smelt so cleanly of wood shavings, and taking up a spokeshave, resumed work on a piece of beechwood.

Dad meant to have the last word and, poking his head into the wheelwright's shop, he said "Know what, Mr Hughes? I reckon all you miserable lot are going to be disappointed. When you get to the Pearly Gates and Saint Peter announces your names, the Lord will say 'Well, you ungrateful people, what have you got to say for yourselves? Here, I put you into a beautiful world and provided plenty of amusement, and what did you do? Why, you went round calling it sinful, and a dreadful vale of tears and doing all you could to stop other people's pleasure."

Evan Hughes bent still lower over his work and plied the spoke-shave faster than before.

"For myself," Dad went on, "I hope that when my time comes, I can go in front of my Maker, stand to attention and say 'Thank you very much, Sir, I have enjoyed my time on earth'!"

CHAPTER SEVEN

MA'S BIKE

MA PRIDED HERSELF on her knowledge of matters mechanical. If a clock took to going fast or slow or stopping altogether, then Ma would lift it off the shelf, put it against her ear, give the thing a good shake then hold it at arm's length.

"I can see I shall have to have a go at you," she would threaten, setting the clock down with a force that set the alarm going. We knew that wretched clock was doomed. Ma had paid three shillings and sixpence for it, too, at some sale. Very fond of sales she was, and bought most of my clothes at them. "Just to for the boy to knock about in, with a bit of alteration."

She would spend hours in taking the clock to pieces, laying each tiny wheel and spindle on a sheet of newspaper. Putting them back again was different. When she had finished, there was always at least one cog left over. "Never mind," Ma would say, smiling, "it goes better without it. Just listen to that tick!"

The fact that the hands were racing round, or perhaps not moving at all, did not worry her. It was the tick which mattered. For Ma was slightly deaf and found any noise reassuring. Sometimes she would provide a playful puppy with a tin in which she had put a pebble. She enjoyed the rattle as much as the puppy did as it rolled the tin around the yard, until my father bellowed from his studio "Boy, go and take that damned tin away from the pup!"

Ma may not have been very successful with her clock repairing, but she was a dab hand where bicycles were concerned. She often boasted that she had been one of the first women in England to ride one. She had even ridden in races and there was a silver-plated cup on the mantelpiece to prove that she had once come in first. This peculiar taste Ma had developed when she helped an older brother in his cycle shop at Harrow. In later years, when motor cars arrived, Uncle Ern turned to them and made quite a lot of money. But, before then, Ma had met my father and married him. She kept her affection for the bike. She could mend a puncture in no time at all, or so it seemed to Dad and me.

Ma really gloried in punctures. This was just as well, since her tyres picked up plenty, what with the granite chippings on the roads and the thorny hedgecuttings that were blown on to them. She would take the bike in both hands and twirl it over so that it rested on the handlebars and saddle. Standing watching, his hands in his pockets, Dad would grin and say "Stronger than she knows, your mother is!"

Then she would whip off the outer cover and pull out the tube so that she could run it through a bowl of water until the puncture revealed itself by emitting air bubbles. Dad and I would watch admiringly as she cleaned the place, applied solution and finally the patch. At last, the blown up tube and cover back in place, the bike standing on its wheels, Ma would push it to and fro and exclaim "There, all ready for another spin!"

"Mind you don't get pinched for scorching!" Dad said to her, on that Saturday after the hound exercise about which I have told you. For there were police traps waiting to catch folks who rode their cycles at reckless speeds. 'scorching' they called it, and the culprit might be fined anything up to five shillings.

Ma said that she would take a chance on that, and then she turned to me. "After we've had dinner, you are coming with me to see Granny Bunting and Aunt Ede, so don't you go running off!"

I was not very pleased at this idea for I had planned to go down to the river with Eric and Freddy to look for moorhens' nests. Spotting the disappointment on my face, Ma added "Then you can play with Pedro, as you boys call him."

I brightened up at this. Pedro wasn't his right name but we called him that after some character in a boy's detective story. He was the son of Ma's sister and Uncle Arthur, her husband, and was about my own age. They all lived at Newport Pagnell, or "Newput" as we pronounced the name, not far from my grandparents at *The Firs*. I liked Pedro, but as Aunt Ede remarked to Ma, "Our Flo, those two boys always get into mischief when your Jack comes here to play."

Dinner was at half-past twelve that Saturday, for Ma was determined to make an early start for Newput. Except when we had visitors, we took our meals in the small kitchen that had once been a baker's oven. In this way, Ma could simply turn in her chair and, without getting off it, reach a pot from the stove. This saved a lot of work and meant that our food was hot.

The main dish was ox cheek. Sometimes it was sheep's head with brain sauce. Having a retired butcher for a father, Ma knew all about cooking the cheapest joints, the things left unsold when the shop closed. The cheek, or several cheeks, had been stewed in a huge, iron saucepan and any left over would go to the beagles whose diet, except for the addition of dogbiscuits, was much the same as our own

There were always plenty of vegetables too, bought for the price of a pint of beer from Poor Arry or Stumper. but no longer from Garge Rudd. For Garge was the man who came once every two weeks before sunup, with a spade and wheelbarrow to empty the privy. Dad used to buy our vegetables from Garge till one evening in the *Dog and Duck* when Dad was paying him for his fortnightly service.

"Whatever do you do with the stuff?" my father wanted to know.

Garge Rudd nodded his head and gave a wise grin. "Ah," he said "there's nothing like a bit 'o 'ome-made for helping things to grow in the garding."

Dad decided then and there to buy our vegetables off someone else: yet even then you couldn't be sure.

The meal came to an end after we had eaten great dollops of that wonderful dish known as spotted dick, plumduff to some. The plates were put down on the floor to be licked by a couple of beagles, old Baggage and one-eyed Dancer, who had been eargerly waiting for this treat, then given a swill in an enamel bowl out in that lofty building, the barn.

Ma pulled on a shapeless felt hat which she had been wearing for the past five years. She always professed to a contempt for clothes, but she was one of those fortunate women who could pull on a couple of old sacks and still look attractive. I think in her case the secret was abounding good health and animal vitality.

My father lit a Woodbine and held open the garden gate for Ma to wheel out the bike. A Rudge Whitworth, it was, and fitted with green strings as dress guards over the back wheel. This was usual with ladies' cycles, otherwise the riders' long skirts and petticoats might get caught up in the spokes and then who knows what might. happen. There was something different about Ma's bike, though. It was fitted with two backsteps, one on either side of the rear hub. This was Ma's own idea and they were for me to put my feet on when I rode on the carrier which had been thoughtfully fitted with a cushion.

"Get up, boy!" said Ma and I perched myself on the carrier, found the backsteps with my feet and clutched her waist. "Let go of me and don't take hold till we get started!" Ma snapped, one foot on a pedal and pushing with the other. "You'll have us both off!"

We were away to a wobbly start that was not helped by Ma having to make a grab at her hat and so leaving only one hand for control of the steering.

Alby and Our Nelly Rudd were sitting on Sal Heffer's doorstep as we wobbled past. Alby picked up a stone and threw it. Our Nelly said "*Cor, look!*" I took one arm from Ma's waist so that I could shake a fist at Alby.

"Keep a tight hold, boy!" Ma shouted and then started laughing quietly with the joy of speed, for now we were really under way and her feet were flying round. I looked back in time to see Sal Heffer chasing Alby and Our Nelly with a broom and to hear her screech "T'ain't right! Risking that poor boy's life. Ought to be reported, she did!"

We spun on through Up End, past the lampost with the letterbox and its new plate of posting times, then down the hill where the little brook tinkled and gurgled its way to join the main river. Past Honeymoon Cottage and the wheelwright's shop where Evan Hughes, looking over his half-door, smiled faintly and half raised a hand before turning round amidst the woodshavings. I guessed he would be shaking his head as he pondered the fate of the sinful who went whirling around the countryside on mechanical contraptions.

As we passed the Grange, I thought of Old Billy and his motor car and wasn't sure which I liked best, riding in that or sitting behind Ma, holding on to her waist for dear life as she pedalled away. When she came to a corner, she rang a little bell attached to the handlebars. *Tingaling, tingaling*, just in case somebody was walking in the middle of the road.

Just before we got to the spot where the Washbrook road joins the one from Bedford and right on the corner, I heard the rat-a-tat of hooves and the crunch of iron-tyred wheels. Ezra Peabody was on his way home in his shandrydan. As we drew near, Ma nodded and called out "Good afternoon, Mr Peabody."

The old chap looked as if he had seen a ghost. He stood up, he pulled on the reins, he shook his whip. "Whoa, whoa!" he piped then, looking over his shoulder after we had passed, he shouted after us "A woman has no business tearing about the countryside a-frightening decent folks's 'orses. Ought to be a law against it, there did!"

Ma chuckled and called out to me "Your father says that man drives around all day to keep out of the way of the bumbailiffs."

We crossed the river by the long North Bridges just before climbing the hill by the church. The chimes were playing *The Ash Grove* as Ma leaned forward in her saddle and strained at the pedals. I knew the tune because we had to sing the song at school. I never could sing a note right though I could recognise tunes. Sometimes, those chimes played *The Minstrel Boy* and that is, I supposed, where Eric had learned it.

Now we were in the High Street. Women with bags and baskets were standing in front of shops and sometimes entering them. Men leaned on their walking sticks, sucked at their pipes and talked loudly to each other. Outside the big, white front of *The Swan*, two farmers regarded the scene. Anyone could see they were gentlemen farmers by their baggy riding breeches and their polished leather leggings.

Except on Market Day, nobody hurried when they went 'up street' in Newput; to have done so would have been almost indecent. A woman put on her best hat and a man his collar and tie to go Up Street. But this fact did not worry Ma as she pedalled merrily along. In our progress from Washbrook, she had lost two hairpins and her hair was shaking loose from the bun in which she had twisted it. A wisp of it was sweeping across my nose and making me sneeze.

We turned off from the High Street close to *The Coachmakers' Arms*, a little pub with a low roof. Dad had told me the landlady's name was Fanny Bunyan and that she was a direct descendant of the man whose statue stands in the middle of Bedford town. At home, we had a couple of books by John Bunyan, bound in leather and gilt. I had never read them. I thought they would be a bit dry. But I had looked at the pictures in one of them of a town called Mansoul, for Grandpa had told me that this was really Newput.

At last we came to the redbrick house where Uncle Arthur and Aunt Ede lived, as well as Pedro and his sister. Aunt Ede was the oldest of Ma's family and not a bit like her. She was a rather house-proud, stay-at-home sort of body, whereas Ma would have a go at anything short of crime just for the fun of it.

"Rode all the way here without getting off!" was Ma's greeting to her sister.

'Oh, our Flo, you don't say, and with that poor boy riding behind you too! Why, if he'd fallen off he might have broken his neck and then you would have said 'whoever would have thought it'!"

I waited to hear no more, for I could see Pedro in the shed at the bottom of the garden and I ran off to join him.

CHAPTER EIGHT

ON TARGET

"WOTCHER!" PEDRO SAID, without looking up from a grubby copy of a boy's magazine. He was sitting on a bench alongside a stack of flowerpots, for Uncle Arthur was fond of his garden. The roof of the shed and one entire side were of glass and there was a musty smell of leaf mould and dry soil.

"Look at this!" Pedro stabbed a page of the magazine with his forefinger.

Bending forward, I stared at a picture, printed in crude colours, of a man floating on wings supported by his own arms.

"Tried to fly, this man did," Pedro said. "Fool fell and killed himself! It says so here."

I picked up the tattered magazine and read the caption under the picture. It seemed that this man had made himself a pair of wings and jumped off a cliff in an attempt to glide. Why shouldn't he, I thought. I supposed it could be done and I was still thinking about this when we heard the voices of Ma and Aunt Ede coming from the house. Aunt Ede was deafer than Ma and used an ear trumpet. Now they were shouting at each other like a bosun and his mate.

"And how's your Tom?" Aunt Ede had never really approved of her sister's marriage to an artist. Why couldn't she have picked someone who went out to work every day like other husbands did? "How's your Tom? Does he still paint pictures and so on? Or does he spend all his time messing about with dogs?"

"Oh, he's doing so well he says before long he'll be able to afford a redheaded typewriter."

"Ooh, our Flo, whatever is that?"

We could hear Ma laughing and her reply "Can't you guess? I told him if he does, I'll tear it out by the roots. The red hair, I mean!"

Pedro got up from the bench and I put down the magazine. "Let's go over to Granny Bunting's." he said and I replied with a nod of the head. We shut the gate quietly behind us but, in any case, the two women were too occupied with their talk to notice us going. The Firs, home of our grandparents, was a rambling house with a big, walled garden and, if you were careful, you could slip in without being seen and there was so much for a boy to do there.

It was not far to The Firs and on the way we passed an old chap who walked very slowly and seemed really to need his walking stick. He had a fleshy growth on the end of his nose like a big strawberry. We boys no longer laughed at him since one had plucked up courage to go up and ask him about "that thing' on his nose. Straightening his back as far as possible, he said "My boy, that was done through being frost-bit in the Crimee!"

After that we no longer laughed at this man who may have fought at Inkerman or the Alma. When, on this Saturday afternoon, Pedro and I passed him, we even touched our foreheads and said "'Ow do?" and the old fellow smiled and gave a rather shaky salute in return.

Ma always referred to Granny Bunting as Old Sarah, because she was her stepmother, but she was really a kindly old girl and good with children, even if they were boys. She had, as we guessed, gone Up Street shopping. So Grandpa Bunting was probably in the snug of the *Red Lion* sipping Irish whiskey and talking of his days in camp as a sergeant of the Royal Bucks Hussars.

At first we amused ourselves by hunting snails and then making them race along the garden path. The winning snail was put amongst Grandpa's lettuces. Any which refused to race by withdrawing into their shells were ceremoniously executed with a big stone.

When we tired of snail racing, we climbed the big fir tree whose branches leaned over the pavement of the street, beyond the garden wall. Above the top of the wall, the tree-trunk divided forming a big cup, lined with fallen leaves and hidden by foliage, as comfortable a little hidey-hole as two boys could wish for. Pedro and I filled our jacket pockets with small stones from the gravel path and climbed the tree.

We had not long to wait. The voices and footsteps of a couple on their way Up Street came nearer and nearer. Our plan of attack had been worked out; Pedro was to be lookout man and give the signal for me to drop the stone. That first couple were lucky. Our timing was bad and the stone fell a full yard behind them, the sound of its impact on the pavement doing no more than make the man half turn his head.

A second and younger couple came next but I overdid the correction to our previous error. This time the stone struck the pavement about two feet in front of the target. Man and the girl on his arm stopped. Both stared upwards into the green mass of the big tree. We held our breaths, I crouched in the fork, Pedro close to the main trunk..

"That's funny," said the young man. "I wonder where that came from?"

"Perhaps a bird dropped it," the girl said, tugging at his arm. "Oh, *do* hurry or there'll be nothing left in the shops!"

In later years, when I was told about the system of gunnery known as 'bracketing,' I realised that this was what I had been doing and that my third attempt should have been on target. It was.

He was Mr Ben Bradshaw, a very public spirited man, as he liked to tell everybody, together with the fact that he was a self-made man. Amongst other things, he was one of the school governors and, every year, he came on the day before we broke up for the summer holidays and made a long speech that soon had us all fidgetting and talking. All about things like Obedience, Respect for our Elders. I don't seem to recall that he added 'and betters,' which was something to be thankful for.

On this sunny Saturday afternoon, Mr Ben Bradshaw also was on his way Up Street. He was wearing a well pressed blue suit with a gold Albert watch chain with links as thick as a ship's anchor cable across his considerable paunch. On his head and cocked slightly forward was a straw boater with a black silk ribbon around the crown

I had selected a pebble slightly bigger than the mere midgets with which I had missed. It was round and polished through contact with the other stones in my pocket. There was a most gratifying *crack* as it hit Mr Ben Bradshaw's straw boater right in the middle before bouncing off.

Mr Ben Bradshaw's head jerked forward as if it had been on a puppet. A sound like that made by a startled pig came from him. He blinked, then remembering his dignity, he straightened himself and put back his head as far as his high, starched collar would allow, and that wasn't far enough to enable him to see us in the tree. Next, he took off his straw hat, examined it carefully and dusted the crown on his elbow.

"Unprecedented, quite unprecedented!" said Mr Ben Bradshaw as he proceeded to walk rather cautiously forward. He had advanced perhaps five paces and we boys were still crouching on our perch when we heard him, in brighter tones, greet Granny. "Ha, good afternoon, Mrs Bunting, I trust I see you well."

So Grandma was home from her shopping and we listened to her conventional reply and then to Mr Ben Bradshaw's amazing tidings. "Do you know, Mrs Bunting, a moment ago I was struck by some mysterious object. On the head, too!"

"Must have been some sort of thunderbolt." Granny remarked, but we who knew her were sure she did not mean it.

Pedro and I listened to the double click of the opening and closing of the gate. "What shall we do?" I asked.

"Give him time to get well clear and Granny time to go into the house," Pedro said.

"Then what?"

"If the old gal sees us she'll know who dropped the stone."

So we stayed up the tree for what seemed like a very long time. I don't know which of us thought of it, but playing at 'burglars' seemed a good idea. We could sneak into The Firs by the back door. I wanted to know what we could pretend to burgle.

"Oh, you know, anything we find, We needn't keep it. Just hide it, pretend like," Pedro said.

Granny was in the pantry as we crept in through the back door and tiptoed along the passage. We passed her wide backside. The kitchen table was stacked with packages and parcels, with bottles and bags. Plainly this was Granny Bunting's shopping. Before we had time to take in details, we heard her leaving the pantry.

"Quick, in here!" hissed Pedro, diving into a small cupboard under the stairs. There we huddled as we listened to the unmistakable sounds of Granny putting on her coat and muttering to herself about forgetting the sugar. We heard her shut the door behind her.

I had an idea. "Let's burgle the shopping!" I said.

Pedro thought that all right. We could keep nipping out and, taking a parcel at a time, bring it into this cupboard. Then when Granny came back, she would think the house had been burgled.

That is what we did. Making a great and unnecessarily furtive show, we brought the packages one at a time and piled them on top of each other in the little, dark cupboard. The last item was a tin of condensed milk which we planted, as a crown, on top of the rest. What we did not realise was that the tin had been opened and that I had placed it there upside down.

We had tired of playing at Burgulars and were back at Aunt Ede's. I think the two sisters had tired of each other's company for they were no longer shouting at one another. I was hoping we would be going soon, when the garden gate slammed and up the path came Granny Bunting with the wrath of hell written across her brow. Pedro and I had forgotten all about dropped stones and burgled shopping.

In through the back door came Granny, ignoring the greetings of both her stepdaughters. She bustled straight up to the table where

Pedro and I were sitting and, reaching out two hands well accustomed to handling children, she took hold of our coat collars and hoisted us out of our chairs.

"*You little devils*!" said Granny Bunting. Strong words indeed for her. Letting go of us, she caught each a swipe on both sides of the head so quickly we had not time to duck the blow. "Messed up all my week's shopping with condensed milk, to say nothing of dropping a tremendous boulder on poor Mr Ben Bradshaw's head!" She went flouncing out of the house without another word.

I was silent as Ma wheeled out her bike and waited while I climbed on to the carrier. But as we whisked along over the North Bridges and past the gate of Woad Farm, she started laughing quietly. "You must have upset Old Sarah, boy!" she called back over her shoulder.

I could think of nothing to say in reply and, even if I had, my words would have been drowned by the noise that came from behind us. I knew what was causing it. One of those marvellous new steam wagons owned by the millers at Olney. When one passed us on the way to or from school, we would run alongside, jump up and try to catch hold of the tailboard. If we succeeded, then we would pull ourselves up until our feet were clear of the road.

The driver's mate, the man who shovelled on the coal, would look out of his cab and, if he saw a boy hanging on behind, throw lumps of coal at him. He never managed to hit us. Letting go always meant landing on your hands and knees on the hard road.

"Cor, Ma," I shouted, proud of my knowledge, "A Sentinel waggon!"

Ma pedalled harder than ever and, as the puffing, steaming monster drew level, she reached out and grabbed the short loop of chain hanging from its tailboard.

Chuffing, steaming, and with sparks flying from the vehicle's short funnel and with occasional stones thrown up by the wheels, we were whirled along behind it. We swung from one side to the other and back again. I could hear Ma laughing.

At first I enjoyed our wild career, but after we had narrowly missed hitting the walls of Sherington Bridge, my nerve began to fail. "Leggo, Ma, *leggo*!" I howled.

Ma laughed again. I yelled again, "Leggo, Ma!"

"Be quiet, you frightened Isaacs and just hang on!" Ma called over here shoulder. "Frightened Iasacs" was the worst name she could call a coward. I don't know from whence she got the expression.

We swung dangerously round the corner where our road deviated from the one to Bedford. By now I was petrified. "*Please* let go, Ma!" I pleaded. Washbrook was now in sight ahead and Ma yielded to my plea.

The next thing I knew, the steam monster was chuffing further and further away and we were sweeping off course. We bumped over the narrow grass verge, the bike reared up as if it had been a horse, and then came down again on top of us as we lay in the ditch, all among many brambles and much dirty water.

CHAPTER NINE

A GAME OF NAP

WHEN I TRIED to help Ma as she pulled the bike out of the ditch, she elbowed me aside. "Just keep out of the way," she said. "If it hadn't been for you, we would have been home by now. *Leggo Ma, indeed!*"

"Your hair is coming down," I said, meaning to be helpful.

Propping the saddle against her hip so that she could use both hands, she proceeded to do things with hairpins, sometimes putting them between her teeth, at others stabbing them into her hair. Then, having driven the last one forcefully home and given a tug to her hat, she exclaimed "There! That will do till we get home. Get up on your perch, there's no time to lose. I promised Miss Peacock I would play cards with her this evening." We were soon on our way again.

Dad emerged from his studio as Ma wheeled her bike along the garden path and I hung about near the gate in the hope of seeing either Eric or Freddy. But both had gone off on some exciting expedition. A grin spread itself across my father's face and he took off his spectacles so that he might wipe them. Having done this with a brightly coloured handkerchief, he put them back on his nose and blinked.

Two bantam hens had flown on to the handlebars of the bike and a third, perched on Ma's shoulder, was chortling into her ear.

"You two look as if you had been in a ditch!" Dad said.

"We have too, and it was all his fault!" Ma pointed round at me, an action that nearly dislodged the bantam hen from her shoulder, "Has Patience started whelping yet?"

"No, but I think it will be any time now."

Ma told him to keep an eye on the little tricoloured beagle bitch, Patience, and to send for her if he thought she was having any difficulty. She was going over to Miss Peacocks' for a game of ha' penny nap after tidying herself up.

Raindrops were now pattering on the porch and splashing on the path. A sudden, gentle shower, but I found a mean glee in thinking that it was wet enough to prevent Eric and Freddy from enjoying themselves when I was not there to share their pleasure. Going in the house, I looked along the volumes of an encyclopedia on a shelf and took one down. Flying machines, that was what I wanted to read about, for Pedro's magazine and the chap who tried to glide were still in my head.

The shower had passed, leaving the slates on Pharaoh's buildings opposite all shiny and pearls of water clinging to thatch eaves. The swifts and sparrows were coming in to roost and I had the book on my knees as I sat close to a window where the light was best. I had got as far as the tragic story of Icarus who made himself a pair of wings but flew too close to the sun so that the wax securing them melted, when I heard my father's voice booming from the barn.

"Jack! Go and ask your mother to come and help Patience with her whelping. Be as quick as you can!"

Putting down the book, I ran out of the house, along the path and across to one of a row of terrace houses on the other side of the street. Ma opened the door when I knocked on it and I went straight into a small room thick with cigarette smoke and the fumes of Scotch whisky. At a table sat the village nurse, The Nuss, in her starched apron and with the ribbons of her official black cap tied under her chin. There was also a sharp featured, little woman in black dress and mob cap, both sparkling with sequins. The veil over her face was lodged on the cigarette between her lips. Both women looked over their playing cards at me.

Miss Peacock seldom talked about her past but it was well known that she had been maid-in-waiting or something to a German princess. Anybody could tell she was a lady by her manner of looking at you and the fact that she always expected to have her own way. Apart from tradesmen, the only regular male caller at that little house was the Roman Catholic priest who came every week on his cycle all the way from Olney. Even now, I never smell Scotch whisky without remembering Miss Peacock. Not that she drank too much of it; she just liked a drop to be in her glass when it was needed. She lived to a healthy old age.

"Dad says will you come quick 'cos Patience is having her pups!"

"*Manners, boy, manners!*" Miss Peacock talked on about saying—"good evening" properly and remembering "please" and "thank you," but nobody was listening. Ma laid down her cards and the Nuss did the same, saying she might be able to help. The Nuss stayed just long enough to straighten her white apron, wipe her pale, watery eyes and say "Sorry to rush off—duty you know!" before following Ma and me out into the village street.

My father met us, "Two so far," he said "and I think there may be two more to come. No troubles as yet."

"Then she's best left alone," the Nuss said, peering into the shallow box in which lay the beagle bitch who was running her long, moist tongue over the damp, squirming body of a newly born puppy. Another puppy made sucking sounds as it pulled at a dug. "An easy delivery and here's another just coming," commented the Nuss in her best professional manner. "Come away and leave her to it."

We all went to a window and looked out. In the garden beside their cottage, the youngest Rudds were making mud pies in a puddle, Alby occasionally tossing a stone into the well that provided the drinking water for three cottages.

"I wonder they don't all die of typhoid," said Dad.

"Survival of the fittest!" said the Nuss with a quiet laugh.

Patience, from her bed in a corner of the room to which she had been moved, gave a sharp yelp and when we went to look we saw she had produced a third puppy. A few minutes later, she completed the litter with a fourth and the Nuss agreed with my parents that there were no more to come. After Ma had given the little bitch a lap of warm milk, the two women went back to their game of halfpenny nap with Miss Peacock. Ma told us afterwards that the old lady took a bit of soothing after, as she put it, having been put second to a dog's delivery. Just when she had picked up a nap hand, too!

I went back to my researches into flight. The paraffin lamp hanging from a beam had been lit for, although the shower had passed, there was still enough low cloud to bring an early dusk. I had got as far as making a rough drawing of the sort of wings on which I reckoned I could float to the ground from a branch of that big elm tree in Winyards field. These could be made out of sacks stretched on stakes. Being Saturday, I could stay up late and work out more details.

Every Saturday night, there was some slight relaxation in Washbrook's three sections. Chuck Turney might take it into his head to vary his customary visit to Down End's *Cobley Arms* by strolling up the hill to *The Dog and Duck* in Up End. He seldom stayed longer than the few minutes needed to drink a pint of Mrs Pawsey's home-brewed beer, glower into the bottom of the empty pot, slam it down as if he owed it a grudge and go stamping out.

On this Saturday, Chuck gave a sort of all-embracing nod of the head as he entered the taproom. He even muttered what sounded like "'ow do." He drank a second pint, too, taking it quite slowly as he had done the first, not in his usual drainlike manner at all.

Dad told us about Chuck when he himself came home, a little more talkative than usual, from *The Dog and Duck*. It seems that Chuck had sat on the settle with his feet in his best boots thrust out in front of him, puffing away at his pipe and staring into the glowing sticks that crackled and blazed in the firegrate. For though the month was April, a bit of a blizzy always made the place look more cheerful, as Mrs Pawsey said, throwing another armful of twigs on. From time to time, Chuck took his clay pipe from between his teeth, smiled and emitted a long breath.

From his seat on the settle opposite, Turnips Thorne watched Chuck. Setting down his own pot, Turnips looked as if he were about to say something but, if that were so, he must have changed his mind, for instead, he picked up the pot again and took a long drink. This may have been because he had little in common with Chuck, he being horsekeeper to Pharaoh Bugbrooke whilst Chuck was Bert Fowler's cowman.

Another visitor to *The Dog and Duck* that Saturday night was Josh Meddlar from Calves End. This was Josh's weekly relapse into sin after spending the rest of the week in the austere surroundings of that painfully respectable part of the village.

Everybody felt sorry for Josh for they knew his wife was an invalid who hadn't been out of her bed, even to obey the calls of nature, for many years. At the end of his day's work (he walked into Newput and back every day) poor old Josh had the housework to do and a meal to cook for his sick wife as well as for himself. Yet he never complained. When he spoke of his wife he sounded as if he was in fact proud of her and her mysterious illness, which had never been diagnosed.

After Josh said something about getting home to his unfortunate wife, my father asked "What really *is* the matter with your wife, Josh?"

Looking very solemn and shaking his head, Josh said, as if he were announcing the imminence of doomsday, "Do you know what the doctor told me, Muster Lloyd?" my father said he had no idea. "Why, he told me as if my wife's 'eart was to stop beating, she'd be dead!" and he went happily away to continue his life of self-sacrifice.

I was still out of bed, absorbed in my ideas of flight, when Dad came home, bringing Ernie Spraggins with him, "Just to have a look at Patience's pups," as he said. As well as his horse dealing, Ernie went in for greyhounds; did a bit of coursing with them, just farmer's walk-up affairs, none of your high-falutin' Waterloo Cup sort. So he knew what a healthy pup should look like. He said Patience's was a good litter though there was one—he picked it up and turned it over—a bitch, he decided, that looked a bit of a dilling. That was the name given to the runt of a sow's litter.

My father looked over towards me. "Up a bit late, isn't he?" he called to Ma, who had gone to fetch a bottle of dandelion wine.

"Won't do him any harm," Ma said. "It's Sunday with no school tomorrow," adding as she set out three glasses, "This is a drop of new stuff. Shouldn't be drunk for another six months really."

"That's all right, Mrs Lloyd, quite all right." Ernie started to giggle. "So long as it's not like that last drop 'o stuff you gave us. Up all night, I was, after that. Mind you, it was real good stuff but my wife said I wasn't to have any more. Not like Harry the Intendance. His missis said he kept her awake all night too, though not because of getting up." Putting a hand to his cheek, he giggled again, "Drop of real good stuff that was and no mistake!"

All three raised their glasses and drank. Ernie spoke in a lower tone and glanced towards me. I pretended to be wrapped up in my studies of a design for a flying machine.

"I saw a funny sight as I was walking through the churchyard last evening after giving Darky, my greyhound, a run. Very funny it was." Ernie looked at my father for encouragement.

"What was that?" asked Dad, eager as ever to hear something amusing.

"Why, there was Totsie Varley having what I called an ecclesiastical mossel."

"A *what*?" Dad wanted to know and Ma stopped pouring the wine.

Ernie giggled, "Well," he went on, "there was Totsie enjoying a morsel of you-know-what in the church porch with one of them young gents from Filstock vicarage. They must've fancied a breath o' fresh air."

Ma said it was time I was in bed. As I undressed, I could hear through the open bedroom window Ernie Spraggins calling "goodnight" and the ring of his steel-tipped boots on the garden path. A barn owl screeched and, above my head as I pulled the bedclothes over me, there came small rustlings and chirpings as the birds of the daytime settled on their perches under the thatch.

There was another sound, a monotonous *tink-tink-tink*, as if water was dripping into a tin lid. Anybody in the village could have told you what was the cause of it. Old Poey had gone home drunk, something he did only about twice a year. His real name was Painter and he had been dubbed with his nickname by devious country nomenclature. I had once asked Eric how this had worked out in Poey's case. "Easy," Eric had said. "Painter, paintpot, pisspot, Poey. See?"

Poey's wife had seen the light, heard the call, as she put it. She did not approve of strong drink and was prime mover in a little sect which gathered together once a week in a room in Calves End to sing improving songs. One of these was 'Water Bright.' I knew, because Eric, Freddy and I had listened to them singing it one evening back in the winter. Then Eric had thrown a stone at the door and we had run away.

On those rare occasions when Poey transgressed from the rules of temperance laid down by his wife, he came back from *The Cobley Arms* in a truly Christian spirit of goodwill towards all men. And women too, including his wife who stood head and shoulders taller than he did and weighed at least two stones more. But Martha Painter would not be party to goings on, even when the goers were married. She resisted her husband's advances so loudly one night that all of Calves End heard her shrill snap "Now then, Poey, I won't have none of it!"

Now Martha had a system that she put into operation as soon as her husband arrived on the doorstep the worse for drink. She presented him with a toy drum that had belonged to their son before he grew up and left home. Poey would meekly take the drum and carry it to the small shed at the bottom of the garden. There he would sit all night, beating the tin drum. The steady *tink-tink-tink* must have had a soporific effect on him. After a time, he would fall asleep with his head between his knees, waking up later and beating the drum again till daylight.

CHAPTER TEN

THE MONTH OF MAY

THE FIRST OF May was an important date in those villages that straggle untidily along the border of Bedfordshire and Bucks. This had nothing to do with Labour Day, a festival as far off as flights across the Atlantic and, as any farm labourer would have told you, just as absurd an idea. No, the first day of that lovely month was noteworthy for far more picturesque and romantic reasons.

Early in the morning, before they went chattering off to Little Arriwig's school, the younger children of Washbrook went "a-Maying," the girls in freshly starched pinnies worn over clean cotton frocks and with gay ribbons round the crowns of their big straw hats, the boys wearing celluloid collars that had been given a special wipe with the dishcloth.

Then the garlands, prepared the evening before, were brought out. These were contrived from any wild flowers which happened to be blooming, the mayflower itself being as yet still in bud. Small parties of three or four children would carry garlands from house to house, stopping to sing in front of those most likely to produce monetary appreciation.

My father, shaving himself with a cut-throat razor, in that draughty building we called the barn, swore at the sound of small feet on the garden path and, as chattering ceased, high piping voices began to chant:

A branch of May I have brought you,
And at your door it stands,
It is but a sprout,
But it's well wrought about
By the work of the good Lord's hands.

This was followed by an expectant pause and I lurked near Dad, hoping for a coin or two so that I could do the magnanimous by giving something to the singers. I watched as he reached for a towel to wipe the lather flecked with blood from his face.

"Cut my chin, drat 'em! It's only the other day they came round carolling. Wouldn't mind so much if they really *sang* instead of making this damned row. Besides, it wouldn't be so bad if they all came together. Tell the little varmints to buzz off!"

The chanting started again. "A branch of May—"

Ma called out from the kitchen, her voice rising above the sizzle of frying bacon. "Go on, don't be mean, Tom! Give the poor kids something!"

"What, and have them go and send the next bunch of urchins? Oh, all right." He dived a hand into his trousers pocket and brought out three pennies, wealth indeed to a country child of those days.

The singing of simple, traditional verses was not the only celebration of May Day. It was another tradition that on that day straw hats could be worn and love-making behind hedgerows officially start.

Whether it was these pagan rites or just the natural, healthy effects of springtime which sparked off the romance between Aggie Lute and Chuck Turney we shall never know. There was no duobt that, whatever it was, this magic feeling had been greatly helped when Aggie was tossed skyhigh by a cow when the animal was being driven by Chuck to an assignation with Pharaoh Bugbrooke's bull.

That memorable event made a deep impression on Chuck. For the rest of the day he could think of little else, even when helping at the cow's nuptials. That evening, in the *Cobley Arms*, the Down

End pub, he felt quite important when everybody there wanted to know just what *had* happened.

In between descriptions of the actual tossing, the violence and height of which grew greater with each repetition, all illustrated with dramatic jerks of a clay pipe, Chuck would become thoughtful, shaking his head and smiling to himself, a rare procedure with this usually morose man. After they had all been told at least three times about the tossing, Chuck began thinking aloud.

"I never knowed as petticoats could be so pretty," he mused, "All white as snow, one a-top of the other and trimmed with Bucks pillow-lace. And her skin under them—pink as a newborn babe's!"

Then, noticing Turnips Thorne nudging Jonas Thickpenny in the ribs and grinning, Chuck went back into his customary dour shell. But he walked home sober that night.

Two days later, news flashed round the village a sight faster than if it had been carried by one of Jonas's homing pigeons. Chuck had been seen, all dressed up in the black suit he kept for Sundays and funerals and with a clean neckerchief, making his way with a bunch of daffodillies to the cottage on the knoll where Aggie Lute was recovering from shock under the watery eye of her old mother.

Chuck was asked inside, but what went on behind the closed door nobody but the three people concerned ever knew. Old Jinny shot barbed questions at Mrs Lute while they waited their turns at the pump, but Mrs Lute was not one to be easily drawn. Even Jinny's statement, delivered in her shrill, rasping voice, brought nothing definite from Aggie's mother. "I 'ears as your Aggie's a-courtin', then."

"Then you knows more'n I do!"

All the same, it was plain to everybody—even to us boys who were more concerned at this time of year with the nesting of birds—that a change had taken place. No longer did Chuck go rolling back to his cottage on a Saturday night roaring out bloodthirsty challenges to unseen enemies; no longer did he stay abed on Sunday mornings only to get up when the pubs opened.

Chuck took to going home on Saturday nights—he lived alone—while still sober and to getting up quite early next morning. He walked about with a strange look on his face and in his pale eyes, but nobody, not even Turnips Thorne or his brother Stumper, ever questioned him about this. For Chuck Turney had a quick temper. As Turnips, who was quite fearless himself, remarked: when Chuck shouted or swore there was nothing to worry about. It was when the lines on those long, lantern jaws of his hardened as he set you with his grey eyes that you had to watch out.

There was a change, too, in Aggie, who suddenly developed an almost warm look on her face with its prominent cheekbones. What was more, she seemed to be taking an interest in the gayer side of life, and she must have done a lot of soul-searching before pinning that little bow on the front of her grey frock, just over the left side of her skinny bosom. Surely, in chapel, Evan Hughes would denounce such a vanity as sinful, perhaps even as a form of idolatry!

Anyhow, it was plain to most of us that there was something between those two. Some of the women said that Aggie was getting a bit above her station, especially when it was known that Mrs William Cobley had asked her to act as parlourmaid when the Lord Lieutenant and his Lady were expected to tea at the Grange.

Although he took the lead at most local functions, Colonel Cobley was not the squire of Washbrook. In fact, there was no squire, the old estate having been broken up, and the manor house pulled down a century or so earlier to settle the cockfighting and gaming debts of the last one. And it may have been because the village had never been squire-ridden within living memory that its inhabitants were so independent in thought and action. In later years, they would have been described as 'bolshy.'

The Colonel himself liked to live modestly and his only self-indulgence was his foxhunting. He loved horses, he loved hounds; he even loved foxes, though slightly less than hounds. He joined in the social side of hunting, as he did those of his many public offices, with some reluctances regarding it as just another duty.

Not so his wife, the statuesque Cornelia Cobley, whose main occupation was the ascent of a rather shaky social ladder. She had climbed perhaps halfway and had seen a chance to set a podgy foot on the next rung when Aggie was called in as temporary parlourmaid with the idea of impressing the Lord Lieutenant and his Lady.

This was not the first time Aggie had been inside the Grange. She had collected baskets of washing there for the attention of her mother who was a dab hand at washing. She had also scrubbed those seemingly endless floors until her bony knees had grown calloused. But a parlourmaid, now that was different!

Mrs Cobley rehearsed Aggie in the things she would be expected to do when the great day came. She carried trays, she opened and closed the door, she even learned to say "yes, ma'am and "no, ma'am" and "thank you, ma'am" at the right times. All seemed set fair for the success of the Great Occasion.

However, the practical habits resulting from a village upbringing and good, earthy country ancestors are not wiped out by a couple of weeks' drilling in unfamiliar ways.

The Lord Lieutenant and his lady had been shown the garden and the horses while Old Billy's working terrier, Turk, nosed around the stables for rats and Cornelia's pom, Poppet, yapped. These things, with the exception of Poppet, whom Old Billy detested, were his province. His town-minded wife did not hunt though she liked to sail into Hunt Balls like an Atlantic liner entering port. Now sweeping into the drawing room, she was in home waters and a hurried glance round assured her that everything was as it should be.

The Royal Worcester tea service, the silver teapot and cream jug, the sugar basin, the slop basin (why didn't someone think of a more elegant name for that?) all were in their proper places.

Standing beneath the portrait of the Colonel's grandfather, who had distinguished himself in the Indian Mutiny, was Aggie, rigid and unsmiling in starched cap and apron.

Satisfaction showed itself in Cornelia's switched-on smile, but she had not allowed for the rustic instincts of Aggie Lute. Having got everybody seated, Cornelia made the customary enquiries about sugar and cream and, having attended to those wants, she lifted the fluted silver teapot that had not been used since Lady Poppleton took tea at the Grange, and that was two years ago.

Perhaps dust had accumulated in the spout since that memorable occasion, or perhaps a scrap of Aggie's polishing rag was blocking it. Whatever the cause, no tea issued from the spout and, after a momentary frown, Cornelia switched on her smile again. "Oh dear!" she exclaimed with a dry laugh.

In two strides of her long, stringy legs, Aggie was across the room. "Give me hold of it, ma'am." said she and, firmly taking the pot from Cornelia's grasp she blew mightily down the silver spout.

Old Billy thought this the funniest thing he had seen for years and so did the Lord Lieutenant and the Lord Lieutenant's Lady, but Cornelia Cobley had to spend the whole of the next day in bed and Doctor Weston drove out twice in his brougham from Newput (at a guinea a visit) before she felt better.

As for poor Aggie, it was quite ten minutes before the enormity of her action dawned upon her and the awful fact that her term as a parlourmaid had come to an end. "Mind you," as she said to her mother between dry sobs, "I knowed as it was only for the time being, like." But in the end, things turned out for the best, as Sal Lute had said they would. For Chuck, coming along with another bunch of flowers from his garden, set about comforting her in his own, blunt way.

Chuck walked out of the cottage in a daze, muttering to himself "Chuck, me boy, you've been and gone and done it! Now you're going to bloodywell marry that gal. Married! Who'd a' thought it? Ah, well, I suppose she can make a good clanger."

He repeated these sentiments to Poor Arry when he met him driving his thin cows to free grazing somewhere. He had to tell somebody. Poor Arry blinked at the sky where the sun was just breaking through a cloud layer, wiped a dewdrop off his weary moustache with the back of his hand and said expressively, "Ah, seem'ly."

CHAPTER ELEVEN

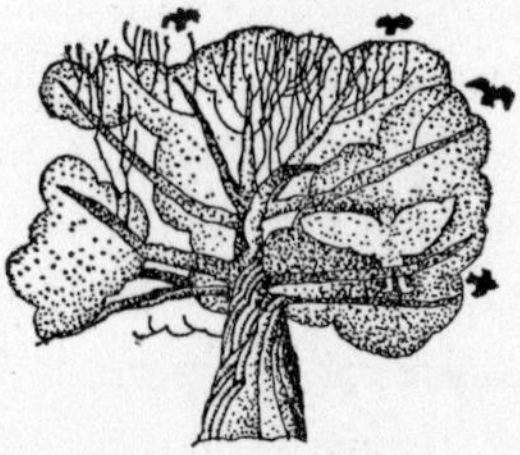

THE FLYING MACHINE

WHEN I TALKED about my plans for flying, or at least, gliding, neither Eric nor Freddy showed their customary enthusiasm for my schemes. Eric said he had promised to go and do a bit of crow-scaring for Fred Fowler. It occurred to me as he walked away, hands in pockets and whistling *The Minstrel Boy*, that this was a funny time of the year to bother about scaring crows off the now growing crops, but I said nothing about it.

Instead, I turned to Freddy. "How about you, Freddy? It could be marvellous. Think of it, jumping out of our tree and sailing through the air!"

Freddy looked at the ground, thoughtfully kicked a stone with the toe of a boot too big for him and pulled at the lobe of his left ear. "Not me," he said. "But if you want to break your bloomin' neck, that's your look out. Only I don't want to be there and take the blame for it." He walked off as if he meant going into Calves End.

I was disappointed in my two chums. Last summer they had helped in hollowing out a rotten tree trunk and in launching it on the pond in Wynyards field after I had shown them pictures of Africans in their dug-out canoes. They had helped me out of the pond, too, after the log had capsized. We had to leave it there when we heard Pharaoh coming into the field. Now, they would have nothing to do with this far more ambitious scheme.

Never mind about Eric and Freddy. I would show them that I could do without them and when someone asked them, later, if they had seen Jack Lloyd's marvellous flying machine, they would have to say no. They would wish they had stayed then, they would. But I still needed help in carrying the machine into Wynyards field. This was not far; only beyond the gate at the top of the lane past our house. However, all was not quite as simple as it appeared. Alongside that gate was Shanny's house and Shanny did not take kindly to what he called "a bunch of noisy kids making a lot of din" on a summer's evening. Perhaps he would understand when I told him that I was on my way to fly.

I thought I had found the help I was looking for in Alby and Our Nellie Rudd. I gave them each two empty sacks to carry, or rather drag, behind them. I myself struggled along with two broomsticks lashed together and two hefty stakes also secured to each other. There were, in addition, two more sacks and Ma's clothes line, a matter which Ma knew nothing about.

We had gone no more than ten paces when Our Nellie tripped over her sack and, lying full sprawl on it, began drumming her feet on the ground and yowling that it was all Jack Lloyd's fault. Alby looked on and made sniffing noises through his nose and, putting out his tongue, tried to lick the end of it.

I heard the sharp tones of Nancy Thorne. "Now then, Jack Lloyd," she admonished, "what mischief are you up to now? I'll tell Nellie's mum who made her fall down!"

While I pretended to take no notice, I could see that, in this manner, I would never transport the sections of my marvellous flying machine all the way to that tree which Eric, Freddy and I regarded as our own special property, even though it stood in the middle of a field of Pharaoh's known as Wynyards. I had a brilliant idea. In some book or another, perhaps one of Fenimore Cooper's, I had read about a method of transport used by American Indians. A *travail*, I thought they had called this arrangement of two poles trailing one end of each on the ground. It occurred to me then as strange that so bright a race never thought of the wheel. Never mind, Henry Ford later made up for this deficiency.

The *travail* scheme worked, though I had to do all the pulling while Alby and Our Nellie walked alongside making incoherent noises. Our Nellie had stopped yowling but she sometimes rubbed her eyes with her knuckles. We came to the gate which was of the usual five barred variety but padlocked. However, with very little help from Alby and none from Our Nellie, I got the poles and sacks into Wynyards and, applying the *travail* system again, dragged them into the middle of the field.

Here there stood a massive elm tree. About ten or twelve feet from the ground, the trunk divided into two parts and with one huge limb extending high above the grass. Had Eric been with me, he would have been up into the green heights of that elm like the nimble monkey he was. And with a bit of pushing from below on my part and pulling from above by Eric, we could have hoisted Freddy up, as we had so often done before. But neither of them was with me. There were only Alby and Our Nellie.

They were no help at all, not even when I assembled my flying machine by pushing the lashed poles through the sacks and thus producing a pair of very clumsy wings. The two only stood and gawped. I tied one end of Ma's clothes line to the crude wings and, tucking the other end through my belt, started climbing the tree. I knew where to find big notches as footholds and then, when high enough, I was able to reach out and grip the branch with my hands. Then it was just a matter of swinging the body until I could get my legs high enough to put them round the branch.

I sat astride the big limb of the elm for long enough to regain my breath before hauling on the clothesline. A struggle was necessary in order to get the wings up to the branch and the contraption had to be straightened out before it could be put to use.

I felt very much alone, perched up there on that bough. The ground was far below and very hard looking. Also Alby and Our Nellie looked so young and childish. Too much so to appreciate what I had come to do. I was thinking of giving up the idea until more and older people could watch. These two would not be capable of doing justice to the amazing spectacle of Jack Lloyd sailing through the air.

Just as I was about to lower the marvellous flying machine to the ground, Alby took his grubby thumb out of the corner of his mouth and said "'E's frit, 'e is!"

Our Nellie acted like an echo. "'E's frit!" she squeaked and then two of them started jumping up and down and chanting "Jack Lloyd's frit, *Jack Lloyd's frit*!"

Of course, no big boy—and when I looked down at those two I felt really big. Naturally, not as big as the Big 'Uns, but big all the same—no big boy could put up with that sort of taunt. Lodging my wings of sacks and poles on the projecting twigs of the branch, I shakily stood up. Then I raised the wings to shoulder height and pushed my head through the gap between two sacks.

I never could remember actually jumping. I may have lost my balance. I just knew that I was falling. As I crashed through the leaves and twigs, I gripped the poles and they must have broken my fall.

After I had disentagled myself from the heap of sacks and the now broken stakes and broomsticks, I looked for Alby and Our Nellie. I expected them to be laughing and that would have been the ultimate humiliation. Instead, they were scampering across Wynyards field, going round by the pond too, perhaps to avoid passing Shanny's house. Alby was making some sort of bumblebee droning noise but Our Nellie was screeching like a barn owl. I felt a little comforted when she tripped over a molehill and showed her not very clean drawers.

Saturday had come round again when Eric, Freddy and I were together once more. We were in Perry Lane on our way to Seven Acres Covert when the rainstorm broke. Freddy said you could tell it was going to come on heavy like by the way that missel thrush was singing and Eric said the bird wasn't called stormcock for nothing. Ah, well, never mind, it was only across one field to Perry

Barn and we could shelter in there till the rain eased off.

We turned up our coat collars and, pulling the peaks of our caps over our eyes, went into a shuffling run, our feet brushing the sparkling water from the grass. The barn, built to give shelter to horses and cattle, was open on one side and with a manger running along the other. There was a loft at one end. Inside, the air smelled of mouldy hay and horses. When we had shaken the water from our caps, we sat on the edge of the manger. We had to jump and, once up, our feet swung clear of the ground.

Eric said there was a kestrel's nest high up in a tree in Seven Acres and, when the rain gave over we would go and have a look at it. Freddy said we might get catched. I kept quiet. So far, nobody had spoken of my attempted flight but there was something about the silence following Freddy's last remark that gave me the idea that the awkward subject was about to be brought up.

Grinning and thoughtfully scratching his nose, Freddy said "They tell me you didn't fly very far then."

I said no, not very far, and Eric slid down to the soiled straw on the floor of the barn. He took a slip of brown paper out of a jacket pocket and, selecting a pile of very dry horsedung, rubbed some between his hands before rolling it in the brown paper. "Makes a lovely cigar," he remarked. While he was lighting it, I asked how Freddy knew about my short aerial trip.

"Our Nellie told me," Freddy replied, but before I could say what I thought of his young sister's help on that occasion, I was interrupted by a violent fit of coughing from Eric. Freddy said to look out or he'd be sick and, the way he was going on with those matches, he'd set the barn on fire. Then he turned to me. "It's all them books you read," he said. "*Flying* indeed! Our mum says as if the Lord had meant us to fly he'd have given us all wings!"

I was about to say something about wheels on our feet too, when Freddy went on "Books, that's what does it. There was that one about knights in armour."

"Oh, Ivanhoe, you mean. That was good."

"Might have got you into trouble, you mean! What with the cardboard clobber you made yourself and that real sword. Our mum said as if Long Bob had seen you chasing our Alby with that sword he'd have had you birched!"

The silence that followed was broken only by more coughing from Eric who was now enveloped in a cloud of smoke. I was thinking of my Ivanhoe phase, now passed together with the elaborate suit of armour that I had made myself out of cardboard, the brown paper casque and the saucepan lid shield. What upset Sal Heffer and Mother Rudd, however, was my arming myself with a sword-bayonet relic of the Franco-Prussian War and threatening to decapitate Alby Rudd when he jeered at my appearance.

Now I was out of my knight errant phase, except for one aspect of it. There seemed still to be room for the knight's lady, a Rowena, but early summer and springing crops all around us may have had something to do with that.

Eric said it had stopped raining—well, very nearly. He threw the charred remains of his home-made cigar out of the barn and on to the wet grass, then gave it a vicious stamp with his heel. We could set out again for Seven Acres Covert.

CHAPTER TWELVE

CLEAN BOOT

WITH OUR HOUNDS, the Washbrook Foot Beagles, as my father called them when away from the village, kennel management was a little sketchy. They were supposed to be kept in a brick building that leaned against the wall of Pharaoh Bugbrooke's stables on the other side of a small yard outside our back door. But, after we had given them their morning exercise and Dad had disappeared into his studio, Ma would often, invite the entire pack into the house. She even built them a rough wooden bench so that they could sit in a row in front of the kitchen stove if the morning was cold.

My father had what he thought was a brilliant idea about summer exercise. He had been reading an article—in *The Field*, I think it was—about bloodhounds hunting what is termed 'clean boot,' that is, following the scent of a man without the use of any form of drag. This sort of idea always came into his head after a glass or two of Ma's home-made wine.

It was on one such evening that he stubbed out his Woodbine, set down his empty glass and called out "Missis, I've just thought of something. When the last hare round here gets itself poached, we'll buy an old Billy goat and hunt that!"

Ma looked up from the book she was reading. "Don't be ridiculous, Tom," she said "hunting the carted goat would turn them into sheep-worriers!" So that was the end of that scheme. The next one connected with the beagles was better received. This was that, as a means of keeping hounds fit in the close season, they should hunt clean boot in the same way as bloodhounds. Dad said that the riotous little devils would hunt anything from a fieldmouse to a hippopotamus if given the chance, so why shouldn't they hunt the boy here?

I was given twenty minutes start, 'law,' as Dad called it, and told to run as far and as fast as I could. Then, when I heard the pack close behind me, I was to hide myself behind a tree. That would find out how clever they were, that would!

The beagles, being familiar with my scent, readily followed it and with a cry that must been heard in the next county. These hunts ended with the merry pack jumping up and licking my face as I squatted on my heels, fussing them and telling them how clever they were. Little did I know then of the trouble I was laying in for myself on the day I went with Eric and Freddy into Seven Acres Covert!

It so happened that my father was away on one of his trips, something or another to do with a horse's portrait, and not due back till late evening. When the rainstorm was over, Ma went across the yard and looked through the kennel window. There she saw a row of canine faces, all with that deceptively pathetic look which beagles, and bassets, assume when they are contemplating some impish trick.

At sight of Ma, the whole pack set up a plaintive wail. "Poor things!" said Ma, in the loud tone in which partially deaf people so often talk to themselves. "Poor things, do you want to come out then?" She opened the kennel door. What she had not done was to make sure that yard gate was properly shut.

The beagles proclaimed their joy at finding themselves free in a wild chorus that was quickly followed by the sounds of slamming doors and gates and the shrill voice of Sal Heffer as she gave her opinion of them Lloyds and their dogs.

In telling the story of the start of that hunt, Ma always said that it

was Dancer who first picked up my scent. She said this proved what a good hound he was and never mind about his curly stern and the fact that he had only one eye. She dismissed too my father's remark that his appearance suggested his grandmother, at a vulnerable season, might have been successfully pursued by a terrier. But then, Ma always had a soft spot for old Dancer.

Anyhow, whichever hound it was that first spoke to my line, the rest of the pack quickly joined in. One pawed open the unfastened gate, they all took the next one, at the end of the garden path, in their stride and were out into the village street.

Accustomed to the company of hunting folk and being a reader of such esoteric publications as *Horse and Hound*, Ma was well versed in the jargon of the chase. So she was able to give a fair account of the start of that hunt on clean boot to my father when he came home later.

"Old Dancer was the first to hit off the line and, almost immediately, the older hounds went to his cry. They must have overrun the line in the village street, for they checked, though only for a moment. Then they wheeled, hit off the line again and ran in full cry up the lane, with young Countess in the lead, right past Shanny's cottage."

Dad wanted to know if Shanny was about and Ma laughed. "Very much about," she said. "The last I saw of him, he was stamping into his house and saying something about getting his gun and shooting those bloody dogs."

While this was happening, my two pals and I were looking into Seven Acres Covert. We were crouched together under a hawthorn bush all green and white with leaves and mayflowers sparkling with moisture from the shower that had passed. Freddy was on his hands and knees sniffing at a smeuse leading into the wood.

"Old Hare?" whispered Eric.

"Fox more likely," hissed Freddy. "I can smell the beggar."

Putting my own nose closer to the long grasses and twigs which had been pushed aside by the frequent passage of some animal, I too could wind that pungent scent which only a fox leaves and which most countrymen find so exciting.

"Our Dad says as it's where a dog fox has cocked his leg that you can smell him." Freddy said but Eric did not agree. He reckoned he could follow a fox by its scent across two fields and it wasn't likely he'd be cocking his leg all the way. And this smeuse was really a hare's. The fox had probably been hunting her. But now the important thing was to get into the wood without being seen and to find the tree with the kestrel's nest before dark. It would never do to walk boldly along the ride: you never knew who might be watching.

Freddy said he could wriggle through the smeuse and, to prove this, he pushed his head in among the thorns. Eric said it was all right for him, being not much bigger than a good sized weasel, but he himself and Jack here would have to look for somewhere else.

We had clambered over a low place in the hedge and were waiting for Freddy to disentangle himself from the clutching thorns when we heard the beagles. Eric said the dogs were extra noisy this evening. Freddy said it sounded as though they had got out and, as he put it, were "tallyhooping all over the place." He was also of the opinion that somebody would report the fact to Long Bob and then Jack's dad would be summonsed. Locked up for it too, more than likely. Might make one of Fred Fowler's cows slip calf. He had three about due.

On this occasion, at any rate, my instinct was superior to that of these two thorough country boys. For it happened that I knew a little more about hounds and hunting, partly through having listened to my parents' conversation, partly through my share in the kennel management, such as it was, of the Washbrook Foot Beagles. And I could tell from the sounds coming to our ears through the still, evening air that our hounds were now hunting. I had another thought too; that I was their quarry.

I kept my thoughts to myself, even when Freddy said it sounded as if "the dogs" were now tallyhooping in Perry Lane. The coolness

between us caused by my attempt at solo flight had only just thawed and I didn't want to start a further freeze. If our present expedition were ruined by my father's pack of beagles hunting up to me in the middle of forbidden territory, then I might never be asked to come on another. But I could not close my ears to the joyful hound chorus that was growing louder as the pack drew nearer. I was sure I could detect the high-pitched, almost terrier, yap of Dancer and had no doubt about that deep *ow, ow, ow-ow* which could come from none other than old Baggage.

I was near to praying that they would lose my scent, check and take themselves off home, when their voices stopped. We had been sneaking through that wood, stepping as quietly as possible between the almost ethereal silver birches, dodging behind the boles of beeches and trying to avoid stepping on fallen branches. We had skipped over the brook that ran, burbling through the middle of the covert and Eric was standing at the foot of a tall beech, looking upwards.

Following the direction of his gaze, I too could see the nest in the topmost branches. As I stared at it, a bird flew off and away, its long, pointed wings a blur of movement.

Eric took a run at the tree trunk, sprang towards it and gripped it with hands and feet in a way that reminded me of Man's simian connections. He was past the lower branches and swinging higher when the hound chorus broke out again. Only now it sounded much nearer. The merry sound was close at hand and being echoed by the trees of Seven Acres Covert.

Above the crackling of dry twigs and rustling of leaves, rang the happy baying of a pack of beagles as they gambolled around Freddy and me. With a look on her face that plainly asked for approval, Baggage pawed me. Young Countess did what she no doubt intended for a triumphal dance and Dancer just sat and howled. The rest lay, rolled or skipped around, but all were contributing to a din that was setting pheasants cock-upping, jays scolding and every blackbird in the wood chattering.

Eric came down out of that beech tree nearly as quickly as I had fallen from "our" elm in my better-forgotten flight. He crashed through the lower branches, landing on hands and knees. Picking himself up and dusting off the leaves and twigs, he urgently hissed "For Christ's sake let's get out of here!"

All caution abandoned, we went along the ride at a run, and quite openly, Eric and I frequently looking round and urging Freddy to make greater efforts. The beagles clustered around me and I was really praying now that they would not hit off the line of fox or hare. I kept talking to them in the sort of tones I had heard used by that red-coated whip with the foxhounds.

I heard the panting of Freddy from somewhere in the rear and saw Eric stop. "You two go on and never mind me!" gasped Freddy.

Eric said not bloomin' likely. We would wait for him. But I dare not wait, knowing the beagles would be straight back into that wood where there were so many wonderful scents.

Later that evening, after I had taken the beagles home and regaled my parents with my story of their hunt on clean boot, Eric, Freddy and I gathered by the light of the lamp-post with its postbox. Freddy wanted to know what my father had said about the hunt. I said he only laughed. "Cor," said Freddy, "if I'd a' told our dad, he'd have give me a ding round the ear'ole."

CHAPTER THIRTEEN

THE RABBIT

WE SQUATTED ON our haunches around the glowing ashes of a tiny stick fire. A big stone was on each side of the fire and, resting on these was a rusty tin lid. Five moorhen's eggs had been broken into the lid and now they were hissing and bubbling like the unholy brew of some evil witch.

"We ought to have boiled them," Freddy said mournfully and shook his head. "This way they'll frizzle to nothing. And all that trouble we had in getting to the nest! My boots are full of water now."

"Then take them off and tip the water out," retorted the ever practical Eric Thorne. " "Our dad says he and our Uncle Stumper always used to cook moorhen's eggs this way."

Freddy snorted. He was the youngest of the three of us and went to Little Arriwig's school. His knowledge of the creatures of the fields and hedgerows was amazing even for a country boy; he could identify birds by their songs though some of the names by which he knew them would not have been found in any natural history book. If he so wished, he could catch almost anything, either by trap, snare or, often, with his bare hands. He would crouch for hours, together with a scraggy cat, by the side of a cornrick watching for the slight twitching of a straw that betrayed the movement of rat or mouse. The following year, he and I went into the mole-catching business together.

The Rudd family lived in one of a pair of thatched cottages opposite our home. There was a batch of four altogether, three of them condemned as unfit for human habitation and due to be pulled down when no longer occupied. That was the real reason my father had been able to buy the lot for a hundred pounds. The actual object of this rash act on his part, or so he always said, was the colour of one of the cottages.

Tory though he was, Dad could never stand Prussian blue as a colour and he said this cottage offended his aesthetic taste and that it must come down. Actually, he never did get round to having the place pulled down or even repainted on the outside. Eric's Uncle Stumper lived there and went on living. As for the colour, Mrs Stumper, a strong-minded woman, said she liked it.

Knowing that I was a pal of Freddy Rudd's, Dad often asked me about the state of their cottage, for which they paid half-a-crown a week rent. He said he was sure something in the way of repairs needed doing, especially with all those kids. He had never realised the size of the family living in that three roomed home until, coming back from morning exercise, he had seen them all pouring out under the loving gaze of their mother. The place was fairly exuding children.

"Why, Mrs Rudd," my father cried, "how ever many have you got?"

"Truth to tell, Muster Lloyd, I dunno. I never took the trouble to count them. And there's three more lying up in the churchyard."

As Dad watched them go down the village street, a laughing, rather grubby but completely happy little mob, he wondered whether Mrs Rudd's vagueness about their number was because this now exceeded the number of fingers on her two hands. In other words, perhaps she could not count beyond ten.

Freddy was the youngest but two of the Rudd family, and not quite the smallest. That was Alby. As Mrs Pyecroft remarked when looking the family over with a critical, animal-breeder's eye, it was like a sow's litters tailing off in number and size when the boar gets a bit old. At the same time, Freddy was not short of brains or imagination.

Dad gave up asking Mrs Rudd if the cottage needed anything doing to it, saying that she would never complain to him. He suggested that I should tackle Freddy on the matter. "He'll talk to you, boy. Anything at all, so long as it's not too big and costly. I expect Ned Varley would take on a bit of plastering or bricklaying for very little money. Just you ask Freddy about it, boy."

The spot where we were frying the eggs was a small quarry from which stone had been dug ages ago to build some place now long forgotten. The men had dug down to the spring bearing greensand and the place had filled with water. High banks, now overgrown with brambles and thorn bushes made it impossible to see from even a few yards away and when we three boys first came upon it, the romance that is somewhere in every boy's make-up, stirred in us.

We would call the place "The Secret Lake" and tell nobody else about it, not even the Big 'Uns, even though they should twist our arms and scrub our chins till we yelled. Here was the perfect headquarters for planning our expeditions.

As we watched the eggs in the tin lid—and they were now frizzling in a very half-hearted manner over the dying embers—I remembered Dad's words about the Rudd home and any possible repairs. With all a young lad's bluntness, I blurted out "Freddy, our Dad says . . ." (Early on, I had adopted the habit of referring to any relation with the prefix "our") "Our Dad says I was to ask you if your mum wants anything doing to the house."

Freddy thought for several minutes and then replied, very slowly, "No, Jack, there ain't nothing."

"Nothing at all? Nothing like a windowpane, like that one you put a stick through back in the winter?"

"No, Jack. Our Dad dinged me alongside the ear'ole and then stuffed an old sack in the window."

"P'raps there's a brick or two out of the wall?"

"Oh, ah, come to think of it, there are three bricks out of the shitus wall, just at the back of the seat and under it. But don't you let your dad put them back! You see, me and our Alby gets no end of fun with a bunch of stinging nettles when our Nellie takes a squat."

The fire's glow was becoming no more than a glimmer and the sizzling of the lid no more than a slight protest. Freddy stared disapprovingly at the mess. I poked a couple of twigs onto what remained of the fire.

"It wants fannywoofing," declared Eric, whose high spirits never failed him. Taking off a big, rather dirty, cloth cap, he made sweeping motions in the direction of the fire and the draught so created raised a small, flickering flame.

"I'll fannywoof you, you mischievous young beggars!" The voice came from behind us, and turning, we saw a big man in breeches and leggings, with a bushy black beard rioting all over his face and a thick ashplant walking stick hooked over an arm. It was Mr Bugbrooke himself, known to us as Pharaoh because of his resemblance to the Egyptian king in a picture hanging in Evan Hughes's workshop.

Freddy and I just went on squatting there, our mouths agape and feeling a little scared, But not the resourceful Eric. "Good evening, Muster Phar—I mean Bugbrooke," said Eric brightly, getting to his feet. "Rum weather we're having!"

Very slowly, Pharaoh took the stick off his left arm and thoughtfully ran a hand along its length. "I'll rum weather you with a stroke across the backside, you impudent young monkey!" he growled.

It is surprising how quickly one can move in an emergency; in calmer moments, I don't think anyone realises just how quickly. After the movements had taken place I even found time to look back over the top of a bramble clump. I saw Pharaoh raise a booted foot and kick ashes, tin lid, eggs and all into the Secret Lake. Then I ran after my two chums.

We ran and walked quickly for three fields, being careful to keep close to the leafy hedgerows and not to move in a straight line. This form of progress was the idea of Eric who explained that we could thus foil any attempt that Pharaoh might make to follow us. Eric had a keen sense of the dramatic and, now and again, he would stop; look round him, hold up a hand and hiss "Sh-sh!"

Freddy, a more down-to-earth sort of chap, did not hide his impatience with these performances. "You don't suppose old Pharaoh is going to bother to follow us, do you?" he demanded.

"You never can tell!" replied Eric. "He'd just like to catch us and give us a welt apiece with that stick of his and then tell Long Bob about us and p'raps have us summonsed." He was about to start whistling and I expected to hear the opening bars of *The Minstrel Boy*. Instead, he unpursed his lips and said "Besides, Freddy, you couldn't run fast enough to get away from him."

Freddy looked down, rather sadly, at the hard, hobnailed leather boots on his small feet. They were at least one size too big for him but he, being one of the young and small members of a large family, had to take turn with clothes and boots handed down from elder brothers.

"It's all very well for you two," Freddy grumbled. "Eric can run a bit and Jack is all arms and legs and goes like a hare. It's these 'ere boots of mine!"

"Don't you worry, Freddy me boy," Eric told him, giving a knowing jerk of the chin. "Me and Jack will stay with you if we get chased."

This heroic statement cheered Freddy a little and he brightly suggested "P'raps if somebody did run us, you could both take hold of my hands and sort of pull me along."

"And so we will, Freddy me boy, so we will!" Eric told him. But now it was Freddy himself who was holding up a hand and motioning for silence. His gaze was on the far bank of a deep ditch. This bank was topped by a hedge where the hawthorn was delicately cloaked with that beautiful, pale shade of green seen only in spring and very early summer. Amongst the hawthorn twined wild rose briars, studded with fierce, curved thorns.

Beneath the thorns and brambles and cowparsley, there sprouted dog's mercury and the hooded blooms of cuckoopint. White wood violets were dotted among the tufts of coarse grass and young nettles. But it was not the botanical details which were holding Freddy's attention.

He stood for a moment or two like a cat about to spring and then, with surprising smoothness and silence, moved on his booted feet to the side of the ditch and dropped into it, landing on his knees in its bone-dry bottom.

"Rabbit!" Freddy hissed, his eyes sparkling. "Went somewhere in here!" He began grubbing with his hands like a digging dog, pulling aside the tufts of grass and other vegetation while Eric and I looked on.

Presently, Freddy thrust an arm into the bank and smiled up at us. "Here it is!" he whispered eagerly. "This is the burrow. Now, if we can only find the bolt-hole!"

Eric dived into the ditch and, kneeling on the bank where brambles clutched at his cap, he examined the ground, his nose only just clearing the vicious young nettles, his hands groping amongst them. "Got it!" he breathed triumphantly, squirming on his stomach among the greenstuff until he also had a hand and arm in the rabbit's burrow, but from the opposite end, thus blocking the occupant's escape route.

Freddy was now sprawled in the ditch, one cheek flattened against the bank as he tried to reach even further into the burrow. "Touched it! Feel fur!"

I looked on, an ignorant novice alongside these two experts who had learned the craft of poaching from their fathers and who had inherited an instinctive knowledge of the ways of wild creatures that went back to the days of the Norman occupation and probably even further.

There was a thudding and bumping from somewhere underground, then Eric was in a kneeling position again but with something furry and alive between his outstretched hands. He had a grip on either end of it and the thing was jerking like a spring so that his arms were moving as though he were playing a concertina. Scrambling to his feet, with the jerking still going on, he released one end of the rabbit and brought the side of his right hand down with a blow that broke its neck instantly.

We admired the still twitching creature with its brown coat shading into greyish white on the underparts as Eric held it by the hindlegs. I remarked that it was a "whopper," but Freddy said it was a bit on the scraggy side and long in the tooth, a proper old buck.

Eric laid the now still carcass on the grass and, taking a penknife out of his jacket, skilfully 'hocked' it, making a small slit between the sinews and the hock of a hindleg and tucking the other hindfoot through his. In this way it was easy to carry or to sling on a stick.

However, this rabbit could not be carried in so bold and simple a fashion; fines or even prison sentences were imposed on anyone caught "trespassing in search of conies" and, always, there loomed the dreaded figure of Long Bob. Besides, like all imaginative boys, we revelled in a touch of drama, even the down-to-earth Freddy.

The resourceful Eric had a length of bagstring in one of his pockets, amongst the penknife, two halfpennies, a scrubby, browning, half-chewed apple and a round pebble. Looping the string through the now joined hindlegs of the dead rabbit, he dropped the still warm, furry body down inside his patched knickerbockers and tied the other end to his braces. Then, putting his hands into his pockets to help support the weight, he started walking and whistling the eternal *Minstrel Boy*. He carried himself with something approaching a swagger.

"Nobody would think I'd got a bloomin' great buck rabbit inside my breeches!" Eric said.

"I would," replied Freddy, "and so would Pharaoh if he came along, and what about Long Bob?"

Eric looked worried but, as we soon learned, his worry had nothing to do with Pharaoh or Long Bob. "What are we going to do with the rabbit when we get it home?" he asked.

"I don't want the thing," said Freddy. "If I was to take it home, our dad would clip me alongside the ear'ole. He won't have no poaching since our Ted was copped. How about you, Jack?"

Having thought of what Ma would say if confronted with the task of skinning and gutting, I said I didn't want it either. Ma was not in the least squeamish about such things but it would interfere with her more interesting activities such as making wine or playing at halfpenny nap with the old girl who lived opposite.

"Then I shall have to take it," Eric said, his expression of satisfaction relaxing his face muscles. Slapping the dead rabbit through the cloth of his knickerbockers, he jammed his hands back into the pockets and led the way along the hedgerow. "We'll get it home all right. What's more, we'll go into the Pheasantry and p'raps have another out of there!"

"When?" I asked, feeling a thrill of promised adventure.

"One evening, if you like. How about it, Freddy?"

"I dunno. You see, our dad says—"

"*Tour dad says*. You aren't frit, are you?"

"Course I ain't frit! All right, I'll come."

CHAPTER FOURTEEN

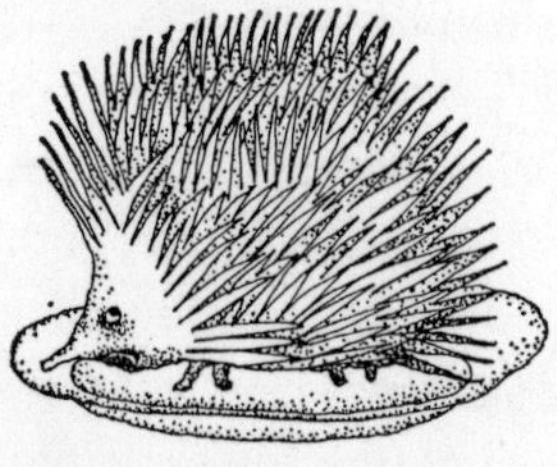

GOINGS ON

AFTERWARDS, NOBODY WAS quite sure who started the goings on in that austere, highly respectable part of Washbrook known as Calves End. Ernie Spraggins told Harry the Intendanace that he couldn't think why it had been so called. Calves? he said, grinning, why if a man hoped to see as much as a gal's ankle there he'd be lucky.

As for who was responsible for the upheaval, Ikey Salt said it was all because of something called Class Distinction and that when the British Working Man had cast off his fetters, whatever they might be, and overthrown the Bosses, all would be sweetness and peace. Then there'd be no need for such goings on. Ikey was the village shoemaker, the snob, and when they used that word it meant just shoemaker and had nothing to do with what Ikey had been saying.

Mrs Potter had no doubt about the cause of the uproar. It was the mother of that scarlet woman down Blackthorn Lane. If only Dolly Varley had stayed where she belonged, in her house of ill repute, then this need never have happened. Mrs Potter told little Miss Fennel, in strictest confidence, of course, but in such a pitch of voice that her words could be heard all over Calves End, that when her son came to see her, she would speak to him about seeing a lawyer.

There was however, one person in that part of Washbrook who said it was a dispen- dispen-something of Providence, that's what it was, a miracle in fact. Josh Meddlar told this to Poor Arry, grazing his cows on Oliver's Piece. Josh said his missis—it was noticable that she was no longer "my poor wife"—was never going to stay in bed again after he himself had got up. No, never no more, he'd see to that, he would! He thoughtfully spat at an anthill and Poor Arry blinked his bleary eyes at the tall elms with their cawing colony of rooks on Hilbury Heights. Then he remarked "seem'ly."

Mind you, there were those who said Matty Miller was at the bottom of it all, but Matty kept his thoughts on the subject to himself. He was a thoroughly contented man was Matty, with tiny gold rings in his ears. As he told us boys, these were to make sure he never went blind. We liked old Matty, I suppose because he was close to nature and because he called no man his master.

Another thing, if a boy was in need of a few coppers, perhaps to replace the perished elastic of his catapult, then he could be sure of at least two pennies by taking a hedgehog to Matty. Just like a sucking pig, he said, after he had roasted it in the ashes of a wood fire. Not that any of us had ever tasted sucking pig. Who would be so extravagant as to kill a young pig when, if allowed to grow, it might weigh fifteen score or more?

How Matty earned a living nobody knew and few enquired. Even Long Bob seemed to keep his prying nose out of Matty's affairs. He had once stopped him and asked questions about some poaching that had been going on but, when it came to an exchange of words, few could get the better of Matty. Anyhow, so lively was the interchange on this occasion that Long Bob never thought of lifting the oilcloth cover off the truck that Matty pushed through all the villages for miles around. To have done so would have meant disarranging the display of bootlaces, buttons, needles, reels of cotton and other such useful articles. Had the constable lifted the cloth, he would have found four fine pheasants from Sir Basil Rossett's preserves.

We liked to find some excuse to go and visit Matty in his cottage, one of a row at the top end of Gun Lane, opposite the *Dog and Duck*.

The thatch of the roof was pockmarked through the nesting of sparrows and starlings and it just might have been renewed once or twice since Cromwell had parked his Train of Artillerie in the lane. That would be round about the same time the Lord Protector saw fit to stable his horses in the church and we knew that was true because you could see where one of them had kicked a chip off the font.

Matty's cottage was dark inside, which made a visit all the more exciting. When you got used to it and when the old chap stirred the fire, its flickering light played on the bare, peeling plaster of the walls and on the two-wheeled truck parked under the steep, narrow stairs. Matty chuckled as he showed us a space behind the chimney breast. "Many a stolen sheep used to be hid in here," he said.

Freddy said that if a man had been catched doing a thing like that, he'd have been summonsed.

"*Summonsed*!" chortled Matty. "*Summonsed*! Why lad, he'd have been hanged by the neck until he was dead." He gripped his own throat with his bony hands and made horrible choking noises, "Yes, and drawn and quartered too!"

Matty was a fisherman as well. He made his own tackle, using a whippy willow wand for a rod and a length of strong thread off his barrow as line. But it was his instinct where wild creatures were concerned that contributed most to his success. He often carried this fishing tackle with him when hawking with his truck. Dad told me it was unlikely that Matty knew why his main occupation was called hawking and that the word came from the old days of falconry when a hawker had a 'cadge' slung from his shoulders on which the birds perched until they were required. Here too was an explanation of the term 'cadger.'

The Great Ouse flows lazily and carelessly through that part of England and, at the time of which I am telling you, it was clean and, in places, very deep. There were willows and alders on the banks and beds of thick-stemmed bullrushes with poker-like heads in the stream. It abounded in fish. Dace and roach darted in silver shoals near the surface, ruddy-flanked perch hovered deeper down, sometimes coming to the surface to snatch an unsuspecting fly while, in the deepest places, huge pike lurked. According to Matty, some of those pike were big and fierce enough to take a man's arm off.

On a certain summer evening, after Matty had sold sufficient pairs of laces and enough reels of cotton to supply him with his modest needs for a week at least, he decided to do a bit of fishing. Wheeling his hawker's truck to the end of a narrow lane, he covered the remaining wares with the loose part of the oilcloth and took his simple rod and line to a bank of the river. He did not go stamping along to the water, but went as cautiously as his forefathers did when stalking a deer. Then he settled himself on the bank, claypipe between stained teeth, to watch the float he had made from a quill of a carrion crow's feather.

He sat there in contentment, watching the erratic flight of a big dragonfly and the dipping of the swallows while he ignored the attentions of the midges. He saw a tiny watershrew go dancing over the wide, flat leaves of the waterbubbles and a fat vole come on to the bank and preen its whiskers within a yard of where he squatted on his haunches. He also saw Squire Knapp of Gayhurst coming striding across the meadow on the other bank.

The Squire came to a spot exactly opposite Matty. He tapped his shoe with his malacca walking stick. He cleared his throat. "Miller!" said he, in the tones of the parade ground.

"Squire," responded Matty, flicking his home-made fishing rod and giving a half nod of the head.

"Miller," said the Squire, allowing his voice to rise a little. "You know these are private waters."

"Do I?"

Squire Knapp's already high colour deepened. "I've warned you before about fishing here!"

Matty made another cast with his primitive tackle and a sly grin spread across his leathery features, Squire Knapp made some incoherent sounds and then barked "Oh, go to hell, Miller!"

"P'raps I will an' all, Squire," Matty said, taking a puff at his pipe, "p'raps I will. But when I get there, I'll tell your old father as you cut down them trees he was so fond of!"

All this happened some time before the event which shook Calves End, just as though one of those thunderbolts like the one which Jinny swore came down her chimney, had struck that corner of Washbrook. If Dolly Varley hadn't decided to take a stroll through Calves End on that particular evening, then none of it need have happened.

Dolly was not a bit what some might call sensitive, but she did appreciate friendliness, people saying it was a fine evening or it was going to rain, that sort of thing when you said 'ow do to them. And there wasn't much of that in Calves End. So why she decided to stroll there on this calm, fine evening, nobody, not even herself, could say.

All was quiet except for the screech of the swooping swifts, the clucking of hens, the lowing of cattle and the tap-tap-tap of Ikey Salt working on the well-worn sole of a boot that he held helpless on his last. Josh Meddlar was stooping to pull up the only weed to be seen in his all too tidy front garden, one ear cocked for the expected call from his poor, bedridden wife. He straightened his back and blinked his eyes as he saw Dolly Varley come sailing into the quiet street.

Sailing is the right word to describe Dolly's entry. She appeared as serenely and silently as a full-rigged ship standing into Falmouth Roads. She was wearing a white dress with a big, pink rose on it and a wide hat with some sort of stuffed bird heavy enough to give it a tilt over her right eye. Later, when emboldened by the freedom that came to him shortly after he saw Dolly, Josh Meddlar shyly gave it as his opinion that she had taken her stays up by an extra tight pull on their laces.

Mrs Potter was just taking the air, as she put it, though Dolly said she had only come out of her front door in order to see what was happening. Her lips were as thin and as tight as the black collar she wore round her skinny throat. Mrs Potter was given to talking about "the late Mr P.," with a glance upwards and the brushing away of an imaginary tear. The funny thing was that nobody could remember Mr Potter although his reputed widow had lived in Washbrook for a number of years.

"'Ow do, Mrs Potter. A lovely evening!" called out Dolly Varley, waving a podgy hand.

The lady addressed, turned half away and, putting her nose in the air, folded her arms and sniffed.

The full-rigged ship backed her foresail and dropped anchor. Dolly swung slowly round till she was facing Mrs Potter squarely. "I said it's a lovely evening."

Mrs Potter addressed a rosebush growing on the edge of her short garden path. "I am particular to whom I speak."

Dolly Varley placed her hands on her full hips and her eyes took in the speaker from screwed-up hair to pointed shoes. Mrs Potter elevated her nose even more and took a step towards her house but Dolly's voice halted her.

"And what have you got to be so stuck up about, I'd like to know! *Missis* Potter, indeed! And what happened to *Muster* Potter, eh? A wonder that son of yours wasn't born pushing a hawker's barrow!"

All at once, everyone who lived in Calves End seemed to be at an open window or in a front garden. Even Ikey Salt had ceased his cobbling. For perhaps two minutes there was complete silence. It was broken by the noisy opening of a casement window which, like those of so many other cottages, had been almost hermetically sealed since it was closed by the first inhabitants.

The spell was broken as all interest switched to the Meddlar home. There, her tousled grey head sticking out of a bedroom window, was Mrs Meddlar, she who had been unable to get up for years and years. "That's right, Dolly my gal, you give it to the stuck up bitch!" she screeched. But Mrs Potter had disappeared into her house and slammed the door behind her.

That is what Josh meant when he spoke of a miracle. What is

more, he saw to it from then on that his wife stayed out of bed and looked after him as a good woman should. And, more than that, he said he didn't care what Calves End thought about it. A miracle, that's what it was.

CHAPTER FIFTEEN

THE PHEASANTRY

ERIC, FREDDY AND I boasted between ourselves that we had been chased off every farm and out of every covert within an hour's walk of Washbrook, every one, that is, except the Pheasantry. This woodland got its name because it belonged to one of the few estates in the county where pheasants were systematically reared and carefully preserved. Sir Basil Rossett, who owned the place, was not very popular with those of his neighbours who preferred the dash and excitement of hunting foxes to the more leisurely, calculated sport of shooting driven pheasants.

It was even rumoured—though some said wrongly—that when Sir Basil's gamekeeper, a morose, heavy-jowled man by the name of Finch, shot a fox he had his wages raised by a shilling a month instead of being sacked on the spot without a reference. Worse still, it was known that Sir Basil occasionally did some hunting in the Shires, where foxes could eat someone else's pheasants.

Sir Basil Rossett and Colonel Cobley sometimes sat together on the Bench, though not if Old Billy could avoid it, and they often met on other official occasions but their association never blossomed into anything warmer than the "Sir Basil" and "Colonel Cobley" forms of address.

I had been very impressed by this distant coolness between these two county bigwigs when I was watching the foxhounds as they drew Seven Acres Covert, back in the winter. Colonel Cobley, the scarlet of his jacket turning to a shade nearer mulberry in places, the nap of his topper staring from thorn snags like a wormy dog's coat, was there on his favourite hunter, a rather aged but very kindly bay mare with a white blaze down the middle of her face. The mare—her name was Molly—was as tense with anticipation as her rider, as both listened to the ringing clamour of hounds rousing a fox in covert. Old Billy was sitting Molly at a corner of the wood away from the rest of the field and he was sure they would see the varmint break covert within the next two minutes.

Sir Basil, looking a trifle too dressy in a new shooting suit, came up on foot. He was there because he wanted everybody who mattered to see that, actually, he approved of hunting. If he had expected Old Billy to greet him with the deference due to his title, then Sir Basil was disappointed.

There was only one thought in Old Billy's head at that moment, a certainty that a movement in the undergrowth was not caused by a hound. He sat his mare like a setter at point.

"Tell me, Colonel," said Sir Basil in a loud voice, "who is at the old hall now?"

Old Billy gripped his whip until the knuckles bulged inside his gloves. He did not take his eyes off that place in the hedge bounding the covert where instinct told him he would see a red mask grinning at him. He did not even grunt in reply.

Not to be put off, Sir Basil enquired in high-pitched tone "Does he preserve?"

The red mask appeared, followed by a lithe, russet-coloured body ending in a white-tagged brush. Old Billy and Molly might have been an equestrian statue, they were so still and silent. Then, after the fox had loped effortlessly and unhurriedly as far as the middle of the field, Old Billy stood up in his stirrups, held his topper on high and screamed out that primitive sound which may well be one of the first cries man ever learned to give and which, spelled "view holloa" is pronounced by all God-fearing foxhunters as "view holler."

If ever there was an example of a perfectly happy man it was Colonel Cobley at that moment. As he shortened Molly's reins and prepared to gallop after the racing pack when they came out of covert, he found time to call back over his shoulder to Sir Basil "Yes, he preserves all right—*foxes*!"

I recalled that incident as the three of us made our way towards the Pheasantry, pausing at Sir Basil's boundary hedge to make sure we had not been seen. Not that we had designs on his pheasants. Even to us, who belonged to the lawless race of boys, pheasants at rearing time were sacred. But we knew there were rabbits in the Pheasantry and, for them, we observed no close season.

I was thinking as we crept quietly towards those tall trees, keeping well into the thick, double hedge that grew right up to them, that if were "catched", as Freddy put it, and hauled in front of the Bench, Sir Basil would show us no mercy.

Now we had come to the spot where the big hedge ended and that dark plantation began. Between us and the trees stood a six feet high fence of wire netting, stretched between steel posts. Even as we looked at it, we saw the fluffy white scuts of three young rabbits go bobbing off into the long grass. We had no eyes for the pheasant poults that were scratching for food deeper in the wood.

"How was that last rabbit you took home?" Freddy whispered.

"The damned thing!" Eric hissed back. "Our mum had no end of a job skining it and, when she did get the skin off, it was all sores underneath. We had to boil it for the hens. What's more, my legs were bitten all over by rabbit fleas!"

"How do we get through this fence?" I wanted to know, while my heart pounded so loudly that I wondered if that was what had frightened the rabbits. "Or do we go under?"

"It's buried a foot in the ground and it goes right round the wood," Eric told us. "We go *over* it!"

Freddy was looking down at his boots and Eric got the message. "Don't you worry, Freddy me boy! I'll give you a leg up."

There was something about that dark wood that filled me with awe, the shade of its trees passing into almost complete darkness and enclosed by the high fence stretched taut between tall posts. The place was like a cage and I could still feel my heart beating.

"Up you go, Jack!" Eric whispered and I was sure he could be heard for at least half a mile. "Then, when you are over, you can catch Freddy if he falls."

Gripping a post with my hands and putting one foot on each side of it, I put my toes in the mesh of the netting and began to climb. Light in weight and long of leg, I was as nimble as a squirrel but my nerve for heights was not as good as Eric's. As I reached the top of the netting and swung a leg over, I heard Freddy protesting that he couldn't do it and Eric's hushed voice telling him that of course he could and not to make such a fuss and noise about it. Anyhow, Eric would give him a shove.

The mesh of the wire was small for the worn toes of Freddy's boots but, grunting and puffing and with Eric pushing from behind, he came slowly up. He teetered on the top and, for a moment, it was uncertain on which side he would fall, but a shove from Eric settled it and he fell on top of me, bringing me down with him all among the bluebells that were a haze about the roots of the trees. Eric came over and down with the same ease which took him to uppermost branches when after the eggs of kestrels or other high-nesting birds.

We crouched low as we peered into the gloom of the wood and then moved in silence until Freddy whispered "Here it is—the rabbit burrow!" Dropping to his knees, he put his hands amongst the long grass, dog's mercury and blubells.

"And here's the bolt-hole!" exclaimed Eric, also on his knees.

"A breeding stop," said Freddy, using the countryman's term for that shallow, short burrow in which a doe rabbit produces and rears her kindle. "If there are young 'uns we could take them home and keep them until they grew big enough to eat. I've got an empty hutch." He did not explain how he was going to deal with any objections that might be raised by "our Dad."

"You take this end," Eric, the organizing brain, said to me, "while Freddy keeps his arm up the one where he is. I am going to keep watch."

Freddy already had an arm and hand in one entrance to the burrow. He was sprawled on his side, his face crushing a mass of bluebells. More cautiously, I lowered my own body and gingerly pushed a hand into the bolt hole. I had heard tales about hands bitten by stoats and even by rats and I lacked the steely nerve of the true poacher.

There was a look of complete absorption on Freddy's face and his breathing was heavy as he tried to reach even further into the rabbit hole. Then a smile spread slowly over his pink face and I knew that he was touching fur.

From several yards' distance, Eric's voice came to us in tones far from a whisper and in an accent which he kept for special occasions, such as that when Pharaoh had surprised us on the shores of the Secret Lake. "Oh, Jack, oh, Freddy me boy, come and help me pick these bootiful vi'lets!"

"What the hell has gone wrong with him?" demanded Freddy, withdrawing his arm and sitting back on his heels. Then he blurted out, quite sincerely, for he was not given to blasphemy "Oh, Christ!" scrambled to his feet and was off towards the wire fence like a badger shambling along in daylight.

I sat up too and looked over my shoulder to where Eric was stooping, pretending to gather flowers. There, bending almost double under the lower branches of a larch, was the thickset figure of Finch, the gamekeeper. A twelve-bore, double barrelled gun was under his arm and a big, black labrador at his heels.

"Vi'lets, is it, you poaching young sods!" growled Finch, swinging his stout legs in their boxcloth gaiters and hissing "Sic 'am, Bracken, boy!"

Eric and I were running side by side and, as we overtook Freddy, he gave us a helpless look, as a drowning man might before he goes down for the third time. We each grabbed one of his hands and dragged him along with us. I could feel the pull as his boots stubbed against tufts. I was conscious too that the keeper's boots were thumping the ground behind us, but I didn't think much of his pace. Bracken, the dog, was different and I could hear the soft patter of his galloping and the swish of his feet through the long grass as well as his panting.

But Bracken had the soft mouth of the best of his race; he was a gun dog not a guard dog and he was running beside us, wagging his well-flagged tail. I could feel his hot breath on my free hand. Bracken did not act on his master's orders to "Get 'em, boy!" and "Hold 'em, lad!" even when these were barked by Finch's voice.

"When I get hold on you, I'll kick your little arses! I know who you are, all right and you'll be summonsed for this!"

Afterwards, we could no more remember how we climbed back over that wirenetting, hauling Freddy with us, than we knew how we got clear of Pharaoh. But we had a clear recollection of the mighty *bang*! of the twelve bore and of the patter of shot on the ground around us.

We ran till we came to Pharaoh's boundary hedge and his shorthorn bullocks raised their heads at the sound of our hurrying feet. We only stopped then because Freddy gasped "I couldn't go no further—not even if the devil was after me, I couldn't!" and sank to the ground.

Even then we looked fearfully back, half expecting to see Finch and Bracken climbing over the last stile, but nothing showed itself there but a cock chaffinch who perched on the top rail and began to chirp his monotonous song. I remembered a favourite joke of country boys. If one has enough cheek, he tells a girl to ask a chaffinch what colour her bottom is, and, always the bird replies "pink, pink, pink."

What a tale I would have to tell my parents, for there were few larks I got up to which I could not recount to them afterwards! If one had been very outrageous, Dad would at first look very serious and then, a few moments later, slap his thigh and roar out a great belly laugh. It didn't greatly matter what I did so long as it made them laugh.

Eric was whistling softly, a sure sign that he was thinking, but Freddy was staring at the ground and pulling up fistfuls of grass to scatter, a sign that he was worried.

"Do you suppose old Finch *does* know who we are?" he asked.

"Shouldn't wonder." replied Eric, going on with *The Minstrel Boy*.

"Then, depend upon it, he'll summons us!" Freddy's voice was husky as he raised his eyes to watch a kestrel hovering in the sky.

"P'raps we'll be given the birch like Kipper was last year for stealing the parson's redcurrants," Eric said brightly. "Sir Basil can't abide poachers."

"He didn't catch us and, anyhow, we didn't have any rabbits on us if he had done!"

"If Colonel Cobley is one of the Beaks" (at moments such as this he was no longer "Old Billy"). P'raps he'll only fine us." I suggested.

"*Fine*!" Eric snorted "And if we were fined, who of us could pay?"

Freddy was not in the least cheered. Plucking grass again, he said slowly, "Our dad says as if anybody was catched in the Pheasantry again they'd be exported."

Home once more, with the beagles baying and the bantams roosting on the beams of the barn, I felt secure. Kit, the big tabby cat purred and flexed his paws on a chair and Ma and my father were sampling the latest matured brew of wine. I must have been laughing to myself, for Dad said "Come on, boy, tell us what you've been up to this time!"

I climbed a ladderback chair to help my description of how we swarmed over the wire fence, but in illustrating the return trip, I capsized the chair and drew a protest from Ma. "Go out with a gang of poachers if you must, but don't smash the furniture when you come home!" I finished my account by telling my parents that Freddy said if we were caught we might be exported.

Instead of the usual roar of laughter from Dad there came only an understanding smile and a shake of the head. "To think," he said "that the old dread of transportation still survives!"

CHAPTER SIXTEEN

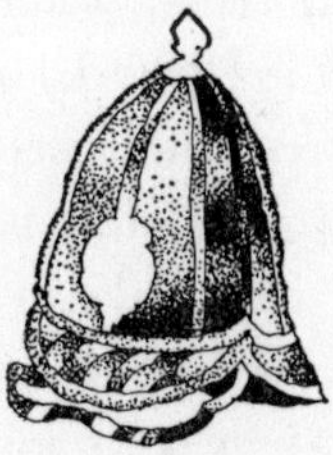

AN IDEA

THE STORY OF our Pheasantry adventure spread amongst the other boys of the village. A few were filled with awe. "Got into the Pheasantry they did. You know, that place up by Hilbury where the boards say 'Trespassers will be persecuted.' They went in though, Eric Thorne, little Freddy and that skinny Jack Lloyd, him with his long legs!"

However, the Big 'Uns betrayed their envy by barbing their remarks with spite. "Get us all into trouble, they will." Petty said to Lanky. "Ought to be reported to your dad they did."

But Lanky, remembering hacks on the shin and a bloody nose, showed no enthusiasm for this suggestion.

"Serve 'em right if they got the birch," Petty went on. The birch was, literally, a sore subject with Lanky and his younger brother, Kipper, for Kipper was the boy birched by order of the court for taking a handful of the parson's redcurrants. And it was Long Bob, the village constable, who had done what he called his duty by charging his own small son, much against the parson's wishes. Indeed, Parson Blossomville had no hand in the matter except in doing all he could to stop the charge. What is more, Long Bob had also flogged poor Kipper with his belt.

For several days I went around with thrills running up and down my spine whenever I thought of the possible consequences of our raid. This excitement became something very close to real fear when I saw Long Bob, in silver-buttoned tunic, walking with constabulary pace up the middle of the street in Up End. His helmet was perched so that its pointed peak nearly rested on his long nose, the black chinstrap was just under the lower lip of an unsmiling mouth and he was heading straight for our front gate.

I scuttled, trembling, into the dark cupboard where I kept my collection of beetles and stuffed field mice and my toy soldiers and I huddled against the half-closed door, my ears cocked.

My father called out, "Halloa, Constable! Come up into the studio. Care for a glass of the Missus's home made wine?"

I crept out of the front door and to a position under the outside staircase leading to Dad's studio, after I had heard the policeman go up there.

I could have shouted with relief when Long Bob stated the reason for his visit, after explaining that he never drank on duty. (I thought —and seldom off it, either). He had come to see Dad about dog licences for the beagles.

Dad remarked that he had six licences, the same as last year and two more than the year before. As my father said this, there was a tumult of baying from the kennels on the other side of the yard. Long Bob observed that there was rather a lot of noise for six little dogs.

"Oh,," I heard my father say casually, "there are quite a few young ones—all under six months, of course, so they don't require licences."

I pictured the constable thoughtfully stroking his thick moustache and then heard him say "Well, I suppose I shall have to take your word for it." I hurriedly busied myself stirring the rainwater in the big butt at a corner of the barn as I heard Long Bob's feet clumping towards the staircase. With one foot on the top rung, he turned and put in a parting shot. "I hope I have no complaints from neighbours about noise, Mr Lloyd. There are laws about public nuisances!"

Afterwards, when telling Ma about the conversation, Dad

remarked that he didn't suppose the great oaf could tell the difference between Baggage, the beagle bitch, and Poppet, Cornelia Cobley's pom.

Our raid on the Pheasantry and even the impending wedding of Chuck Turney and Aggie Lute were both forgotten in the excitement stirred up by my father's latest idea.

Dad often had ideas—without them he never could have painted original pictures. These usually came to him when he was sitting in front of his easel or the desk at which he did his line drawings, with a glass of home made wine close to his elbow.

There had been the sea serpent idea, but that had, literally, sunk before it deceived anyone. The hidden treasure hoax had come off brilliantly, but there was some threat to do with Treasure Trove. This latest idea was quite different. There should be a village show and he, himself, was the man to organise it.

He told his friend, Parson Blossomville, about this momentous scheme. The parson was a man with a broad outlook and tolerant good humour of someone who has travelled far with an open mind. In the hare-hunting season he whipped-in to our beagles and his daughter, Mary, walked a couple of puppies. After William Heffer's funeral, Old Jinny whispered to Evan Hughes that Parson Blossomville had worn his surplice over hunting clothes. The good wheelwright raised his eyes towards Heaven, waggled a long finger and declaimed in a sonorous voice "to think that a servant of the Lord should cloak the raiment of folly with the mantle of hypocrisy!"

When, over glasses of Ma's prime elderberry, Dad told the parson about his idea for a village show, the latter agreed that it was a wonderful thought. "It might instil a little more community spirit into folk, in place of so much sectarian spite. But it is going to be awful hard to get the villagers to do anything to help in running it. Anyhow, I would like to see somebody make the attempt; a show would liven up this village, and Lord knows it needs it at times. Why, I remember when I was staying in Austria as an undergrad. . ."

The parson's adventures in Austria, related in an undertone, were lost to my ears, straining though they were as I pretended to read a book in a corner. He spoke much more loudly when he said "Need a hardworking secretary, naturally."

Stroking his wide, double chin, my father wondered who would be the most suitable man for that job. The parson grinned and looked at him with bright, steady eyes from under thick, upsweeping brows. "There's only one man to do the job—the one whose idea it was in the first place—you!"

So it was that Dad set about organising a village show. Fresh thoughts on the subject would come to him as he was painting pictures of hounds and horses and scarlet-coated riders. He would lay down brushes and palette, walk to the double door of the studio, the top half of which was always open except in the coldest of weather, and take the partly smoked Woodbine from his lips.

"Missis! I've got another idea. How about a baby show?"

"Who would you get to judge it?" Ma shouted back from the small kitchen that was beneath the studio.

"The Nuss. She's an intelligent woman with a real interest in the health of the young. And, damn it all, she helped to bring most of them into the world! *You* play cards with her, so you can ask her."

"She'd never do it. She would be accused of personal bias."

"What, do you think she'd give the prizes to those who had arrived with the least bother? Well, think of someone else then," Replacing the fag, Dad went back to his easel, but for only a few minutes. Leaning over the lower half of the door again, he boomed "Missis! We could have a greased pig to be raced for by the women. Allow the pig plenty of law—give it a long start—and the one who catches and holds it, keeps the pig."

"You'd have the cruelty people after you. Anyhow, where are you going to get the pig?"

"Some sporting farmer would give one. Pharaoh Bugbrooke might."

"*What*? That miserable old devil! He never gave anything away in his life, not even the dirt out of his eye."

Recruiting a committee to run the show was no easy task. Plenty were ready to criticize my father's ideas and some to decry the whole thing, but few were willing to serve. Stumper Thorne said nothing ever "went" in Washbrook and nothing ever would go, but his younger brother, Turnips, after some persuasion and a few pints of beer, agreed to help on condition that a knife and fork tea was provided free for committee members.

Tom Barnes, the blacksmith, as well as Bill, his hefty son, were almost enthusiastic and Harry the Intendance Man said "My dear sir, you can count on my utmost co-operation." Little Arriwig tweaked his ginger moustache and rubbed his hands together. "Splendid, splendid," he exclaimed when Dad asked for his help. "Of course, anything I can do—on the committee, on the day itself—anything at all."

"I knew you would!" Dad cried delightedly. "Naturally there will be children's sports, running, jumping, skipping races for girls and so on. Perhaps I could leave those to you."

"Certainly, Mr Lloyd, with the greatest of pleasure." Although we children made fun of Little Arriwig—as we did of almost everybody—he had a genuine love for young people. "If I may make a suggestion," he went on "couldn't we have a competition for the best arrangement of wild flowers—for school children, of course?"

Coming across Poor Arry minding his cows as they grazed the roadside at the public's expense, Dad mentioned the show to him, not with any hope of help but to test the general opinion. "You see," my father commented, "it would brighten village life a bit."

Out of his watery eyes, Poor Arry stared towards the heights beyond Hilbury. "Ah," he declared eloquently "ah, seem'ly".

If Poor Arry's recations were predictable, so also were those of Evan Hughes when, again at morning exercise with the beagles, Dad stopped in front of the wheelwright's shop. "Morning, Mr Hughes. Going to be a beautiful day!"

Evan looked up from the hub of a wheel he was making to replace one which had collapsed on a cart of Mrs Pyecroft's through age and overloading. He was a superb craftsman and he ran his hand almost lovingly over the smooth surface of the wood before replying to my father's greeting. "And a very good day to you, Mr Lloyd. We must endure in humbleness what the Lord chooseth to send us."

"Amen" said Dad, probably quite seriously, for he professed a great respect for anyone's religious convictions, whatever they might be and as long as they were not pushed down his own throat, as he said. "Have you heard, Mr Hughes, that we are going to hold a show in the village?"

"Tidings have reached my ears of this proposed frivolity" Evan said, shaking his head slowly. My father was thinking out some reply which would shock him when the wheelwright added "but maybe it is the Lord's will that His people should gladden their hearts and so brighten their brief sojourn in this vale of tears."

Evan's statement took the wind out of my father's sails and, to hide his loss for words, he flicked his whiplash at Dancer, the one-eyed, eighth-season doghound, who was cocking a leg against the wheelwright's doorpost.

"I might even see my way clear to giving a prize for the children's sports," said Evan, the flicker of a smile lighting his innocent face. "Perhaps some improving book by Samuel Smiles, John Bunyan, or another worthy man."

CHAPTER SEVENTEEN

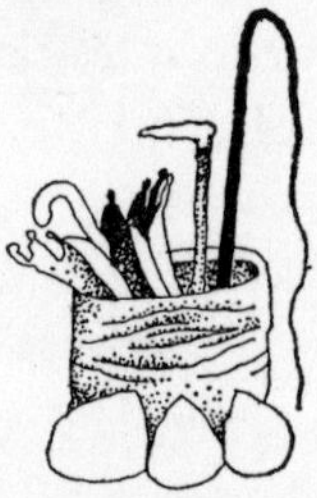

CAPTAIN JOE

Tomorrow's the Fair
And I shall be there,
Stuffing my guts
With gingerbread nuts—
and I can't remember the last line.

SO CHANTED NANCY THORNE monotonously for at least two weeks before Midsummer's Day, the date of that great, annual feast, Newput Long Fair. Actually, the fair went on for two whole days and had been established by statute many centuries earlier. So it was a proper statty fair, coming at exactly the right time of year.

The mowing grass, a chance mixture of fescue and cocksfoot with some quaker grass for good measure, had been cut, made into hay and carried. The two-horse teams had drawn the mowing machines with their whirring knives round and round the fields, the long crop, dark green at the tips and growing paler towards the roots, had gone down in tidy swathes. There it had lain, the sprinkling of purple vetch and pink clover flowers wilting in the strong sunshine, leaving the voles to go scuttling into their newly exposed burrows.

Then teams of men and women came with pitchforks and long-handled wooden rakes to turn the swathes after the sun had dried one side of the cut grass. They laughed and chatted as they worked at that deceptive pace which looks so slow until you try to keep up with it for hour after hour. At bavor time and again at tea-time, cans of hot tea and baskets of buttered bread and jam had been sent out to the hay fields from the farmhouse.

All the while the sky was anxiously watched. If only this dry, warm weather would last until the hay was properly made and carried! And that year brought one of those long, hot summers about which the old folk are so fond of reminding us. Fred Fowler, Mrs Pyecroft and Pharaoh Bugbrooke were able to send their horses and carts to bring in loads of beautiful and fragrant hay without a suspicion of the dampness which, when contained, may produce enough heat to fire a rick. It was the sort of hay which begs to be rolled in.

Now the hay was stacked and the ricks thatched with straw. Here, Stumper Thorne came into his own. It was said that no man for miles around was Stumper's equal when it came to thatching a rick.

The corn crops were growing taller with the passing of each warm and drowsy day. When a light, caressing breeze sprang up and moved over the surface of the fields, Ikey Salt, who had been at sea in his time, said he was reminded of a tide breaking on a gently shelving beach.

There were still cows to be milked twice a day, come Saturday, Sunday or any other day, and the hardworked horses to be fed, groomed and watered. The sheep were now little trouble, their lambs well grown, so long as fences were kept up so they could not stray.

What better time to hold a statty fair?

We boys who went to school in Newput, ate our breakfasts in a hurry and set off early on our walk to that town on the first morning of Long Fair. That way we had time to watch the stalls going up and the building of the mighty roundabout with the titanic steam engine in its middle. There was much bolting and tightening of nuts and great driving in of steel stakes by swarthy faced men with colourful neckerchiefs and smooth, black hats. You could tell they had done this sort of thing lots of times before by the silent way they set about it.

Right down the wide High Street the Fair stretched, right from near Cannon Corner, past the Market Square and beyond the Masonic Hall. Our minds full of wonderful things that would be happening that evening, we were late at school. Little was said by the teachers for the headmaster was an understanding man named O. H. Bull. He had a great love for young people and taught me, in time, a love of my native tongue and to swim.

Long Fair Day was outstanding too for Captain Joe Bagley, Squire of Long Gifford. Joe, not short of a shilling when one was needed, lived in a modest state, keeping up an establishment worthy of a gentleman who had been in the Blues. In accordance with family tradition, he had gone into the Army while his brother had entered the Church. Neither had married.

A week before Long Fair, Joe had his clerical brother to stay with him and, this being a somewhat rare occurrence since his brother's living was in Northumberland or some other such outlandish part, they had "done themselves proud" as Joe's housekeeper put it.

They were a discreet lot, those villagers of Long Gifford and not given to tittle-tattle. Besides, why shouldn't Captain Joe celebrate when he was entertaining his brother? Him captain of the village cricket team too, and his brother a man of the cloth. All the same, there were whispers of what went on at Joe's home, Gifford Manor, on the last night of his brother's stay. It may be that Joe's housekeeper did not keep as still a tongue as she might have done.

The brothers dined well, perhaps a little too well. They were becoming extra meticulous when they spoke to each other as the port was passed and the brandy poured. The churchman addressed the soldier as "Captain Joseph Bagley" and the soldier the churchman as "Reverend Kitely Bagley."

The night was soft and warm and moonless. Somewhere, a nightingale was trilling and bats were hawking midges when the parson left the table and went outside to stretch his legs, as he put it. With the lights of the house behind him, he lost his bearings and strayed into the kitchen garden where he was overcome by a sudden drowsiness and subsided amongst the rows of young cabbages.

It was whispered amongst the more discreet villagers that, for the remainder of that night, they could hear the voice of Captain Joe, as he paced the garden path, declaiming plaintively, "Reverend Kitely Bagley, where are you? Reverend Kitely Bagley, where are you? Reverend Kitely Bagley, where are you?"

Joe received no reply for the Reverend Kitely Bagley was sleeping soundly amongst the cabbages.

However, Joe was over the impact of his brother's visit by the time Newput Long Fair came round but another shock was to overtake him on that Midsummer's Day, though it well may be that he accepted the event as no shock at all. Indeed, when a man has lived as Joe Bagley had done and passed his eightieth year, he has usually developed an attitude towards life which acts as a sort of armour plating. So when he noticed that Mrs Bastwick, his housekeeper, was in tears when she brought in a fresh pot of coffee at breakfast, he tried to comfort her. Wiping his lips with his napkin, Joe told her not to worry whatever the trouble was, even if she had knocked the Ming horse off the mantelpiece when dusitng.

Oh, it was worse than that, sir, much worse, and Mrs Bastwick dabbed her eyes with a corner of her apron and her full bosom heaved above her restricting whaleboned corset. She was, she announced, going to have a baby.

Captain Joe cleared his throat loudly and asked who the father might be. His housekeeper stopped dabbing her eyes and said "Why, it's you, sir! Who else should it be?"

The Squire of Long Gifford held out his cup for Mrs Bastwick to fill again with coffee. When he had thoughtfully drunk this, he said "Tell the stableboy to tell the groom to shut the blood mare in the gig." In that part of the country, a horse is always "shut in" to shafts.

After Captain Joe had attended to a few small matters some connected with the estate, he pulled on one of those garments known as a covert coat and took a round-topped, tall hat from a peg in the hall. Then, having selected a gig whip from a stand made from an elephant's foot, he strode out of the front door.

A ratfaced lad in shirtsleeves was holding the head of a breedy little mare who was too fond of showing the white of her eye. Ernie Spraggins had picked her up at Stow-on-the-Wold horse fair and, spotting her uncertain temper, had quickly sold her to the Captain who, he knew, liked a horse or a woman with a bit of spirit. Now the mare was between the shafts of a yellow-wheeled, high-seated gig, though whether the vehicle was a Whiskey, a Newport Pagnell or some other variety, nobody seemed to know, least of all the ratfaced lad.

When she saw Joe, the mare pricked her ears and whinnied. Taking the reins, Joe put a foot on the step and swung up into the seat with an ease a far younger man might have envied. The lad was now having to fight to keep hold of the mare.

"All right, Sam!" called out Joe and, releasing his hold, the lad jumped out of danger.

The mare was off like a fox from his earth when there is a good terrier yapping at his brush. The yellow wheels spun round, Joe jammed on his tall hat and gave a twirl to the whiplash. Out between the two stone gateposts with a talbot supporting a shield on each, to swing round into the road. Then it was *rat-a-tat* of hooves and sparks flying as steel shoe struck road flint, and the sussuration of wheels with well-greased axles.

Over the hump-backed bridge spanning the New Navigation Canal, the Cut, on past the turn to Kickles Farm. A Welsh collie bitch darted out from a gateway in the lightning like way of her kind and snapped at the mare's heels until Captain Joe discouraged her with an accurate flick of the whiplash. Men stopped their work by the roadside, women ceased their gossiping over the front gates. "Here comes Captain Joe!" they said or, if they could not get the words out in time, "there goes Captain Joe!" As he passed the police station, the sergeant remarked to the Inspector that Captain Bagley was looking uncommon pleased with himself.

Joe had steadied the mare to a fast trot in Newput High Street, now a mass of stalls, caravans, high swings and other amusements. They were level with a garish roundabout. 'Thurston's Galloping Horses' was painted right round its canopy and the whole thing was turning very slowly as it was being tested. The galloping horses were proceeding at a very leisurely pace and the intricate steam organ was not yet playing. But the safety valve on the mighty engine was hissing steam. A man wearing a waistcoat and a red neckerchief was using an oilcan on vital spots of the engine and he chose this moment to try out the whistle. He pulled on a cord and a banshee screech roused the Crimea veteran from his dreams of Balaclava.

Joe's mare took the bit between her teeth and broke into a gallop. A woman cursed Joe in Romany as one wheel of the gig knocked over a row of cokernuts on iron posts. The mare knew her way to *The Swan* and the good oats the ostler there gave her and she willingly allowed her driver to steer her under the arch and into the yard. It mattered not that they had taken the turn on one yellow wheel, nor that Joe had had to grip the side of the gig seat in order to stay on board; they had arrived.

Joe tossed the reins to the ostler who touched his forehead and patted the mare's neck. "Shut her out, give her a rub down and a feed of oats. She deserves it." Climbing out of the gig, Joe stretched his legs and then strode into *The Swan*. Straight through the entrance hall he went, with the foxes masks as well as a fine pair of fallow deer antlers which, almost certainly, had come from Woburn. He went into the Snug where hung a set of cockfighting prints and where there now sat a few privileged men known to the barmaid as "The Regulars."

Ernie Spraggins was one of them, and it was through him that we heard the story. Dudley Garner too, the foxhunting farmer who sometimes could be persuaded to sing stirring ballads in a fine tenor voice, as well as two or three more. Ernie was wondering whether to ask after the health of the little blood mare when Captain Joe Bagley, standing feet wide apart, in the middle of the little room, proclaimed "Drink up, gentlemen. Drink up and charge your glasses again!"

There was raising of elbows and emptying of glasses and then the barmaid, who looked the sort who would step out sound in the morning, as Ernie put it, refilled the glasses.

"And to what, Captain, do we drink?" asked Dudley Garner.

"Gentlemen," said Joe, "you will kindly drink to Old Joe Bagley, eighty-three not out!"

CHAPTER EIGHTEEN

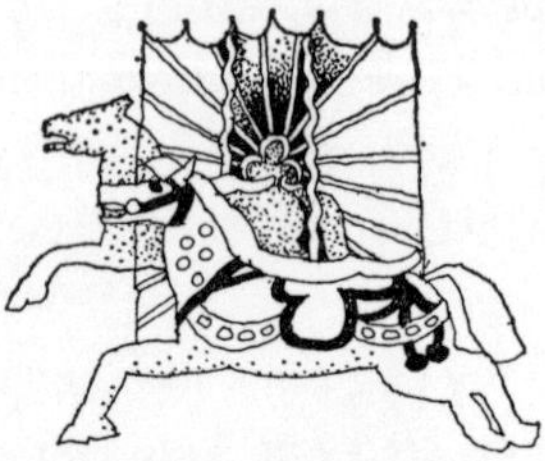

LONG FAIR

MA HAD GIVEN me sixpence to spend at the Fair. In the world of a village boy whose common currency when dealing with his friends was the fag card, this was almost a fortune. The exchange rate at that time was five *clean* cigarette cards to a halfpenny. That was the exact price I had paid Waggle for the live hedgehog he had brought me and which now spent its days in sleeping in a corner where our garden wall met Pharaoh's stables, and his nights in scuttling and snuffling near enough to their kennel to set the beagles baying.

Dad swore he'd settle the hash of that damned hedgepig if only he could catch it and what the devil was I thinking about having such a creature as a pet? I had known an anxious five minutes one moonlit night as I watched from my bedroom window. There was Dad, an animated bell tent in a vast flannel nightshirt, running barefoot and swearing round and round the kennel yard as he brandished a spade at my hedgehog.

That was when I learned how swift and nimble a hedgehog can be. Dad gave up the chase at last and I had an idea I could hear a rumble of almost silent laughter, for he had that happy, if sometimes compromising, gift of being able to laugh at himself. When, at breakfast next morning, he asked where Hodge spent his daylight hours, I shook my head and said I had no idea.

Not that the hedgehog has anything to do with Long Fair except to emphasise the value of sixpence which was the equal of sixty clean fag cards and goodness knows how many dirty or dogeared ones.

Ma said I was not to use any of the money for buying fairings for anybody but to spend it on myself. She remembered the fairings her brothers had brought home from Long Fair when she was a child. Unbelievably hideous china dogs and grotesque men and women on impossible horses. I had seen them grinning from a mantelpiece at The Firs. Grandma Bunting was very proud of them. She would point them out to visitors and name the giver of each.

"My Fred gave me this dog, isn't it lovely? And my Albert this beautiful lady on a horse. All fairings, you know."

I noticed that Ma's name was never mentioned in this connection. But then she was not one who worried much about her relatives.

The sixpence was in three pennies and six halfpennies and all through lesson time I kept putting a hand into the left side pcoket of my shorts to make sure they were still there. Twice, the teacher gave me a sharp rap over the knuckles and snapped out that I was to stop playing with myself. I got another rap too for not paying attention to the lesson.

My thoughts were on how I would spend those coppers. I would ride on one of Thurston's Galloping Horses. That would be one penny gone. Then I might spend another penny on the swings. There was a snag to this however. Two of you were needed to make the wooden boat really sail high when you both pulled on the loose ropes. I thought of Eric who, being a few months older and a fair bit sharper, was in a higher class than I. No, he wouldn't do. He would want to make the boat sail so high that we would each, in turn, be able to look over the top bar and I didn't like the thought of that.

I shared a desk with a quiet boy named Walter. He didn't seem to have another name; at least, if he did, none of the rest of us ever remembered hearing it. Walter wore a jacket and knickerbockers of brown corduroy and, even now, whenever I smell corduroy, I think of him. He only spoke when he was spoken to and never did anything wrong. Somehow, he reminded me of Pharaoh Bugbrooke's mongrel dog Carlo that would tuck in its tail and cringe when his master looked at him out of those bright, dark eyes of his.

Walter was one of a party of boys in brown corduroy suits and girls in brown fustian dresses who walked to school from that stark, redbrick building a mile out on the London road. They were known as the Work'us Kids and they always hurried back to that institution when school was over. There was no stopping on the road to play for them. As Walter said, if they were as much as two minutes late. then they "got the stick." I liked Walter.

Waiting till the teacher had his back towards the class while he chalked on the blackboard, I whispered to Walter "Are you going to the Fair?" then, remembering the rules of the place where he lived, wished I hadn't said it.

A smile like that of someone beholding the world's first morning lit the boy's face. The Work'us Master had told the children they could be a full half-hour late if they wanted to see Long Fair. I asked if he was going on the swings. Walter said no, he was just going to have a look. It cost a penny to go on anything and Walter hadn't got a penny. There was no resentment in his voice and he still smiled.

Walter never had had a penny but there was no envy in him for those who did have one or perhaps, like me at the time, several. I wondered then if the singing of a certain hymn he had told me about of which the Work'us Master was very fond had anything to do with his attitude. Something about "keeping us in our proper stations." Now, you'd never catch the man we boys called "Old Bull," our own headmaster, teaching us to sing that sort of nonsense. He was more likely to tell us there was nothing to stop a boy from bettering his station, nothing that is except lack of effort.

Old Bull let us out of school half-an-hour early and laughed as he thought of what the Inspector would say if he came to hear about it, and all because it was Long Fair. Eric had run off, saying he was going to win himself a cokernut on the shy before Young Poey spoiled every boy's chances by knocking so many that him and his pals were barred. Although Young Poey never did learn to write more than his own name he was a dead shot with a stone or a ball. He could throw a stone from ten yards' distance and cut the head off a sitting blackbird which was a cruel thing to do but clever all the same. Last year, the man who collected the pennies had given Young Poey sixpence to keep away from his stall.

I found myself standing beside Walter who said he had never been to a fair before. I was glad to wait until the Big' Uns had gone. They were always extra noisy and extra big at the Fair. Again, I fingered the money in my pocket. It seemed an awful lot. Taking out my hand with two pennies in it, I sought one of Walter's and pushed the coins between his clammy fingers.

Walter started as if he had been pricked, "No!" he cried, "no!"

"It's all right, Walter," I said "I don't want them."

He turned the two pennies over and over and then thrust one of them back at me. "Not two," he said. "There isn't time to spend two, and if I take anything back, the Master will say I've stolen it and give me the stick."

"Come on, Walter, let's have a ride on the horses!"

Thurston's Galloping Horses were careering round at their best pace, all staring eyes and great teeth, round and round that marvellous steam organ where little men popped out and clanged cymbals and music blared from the pipes. Every now and then, the man standing by the engine with all its shining brasswork, pulled a string and a mighty toot-toot sounded.

Toot-toot, and the swirling and the up-and-down motion of the prancing horses stopped. I felt my heart beating as fast as it did before I had gone into the Pheasantry. "Come on, Walter, let's have a ride!" I called, but the Work'us boy drew back. "I'm frit," he said. "I'll just buy myself a pennorth of humbugs and eat them on the way home." As I mounted the steps of the roundabout he melted into the crowd.

I chose a grand, grey horse and nervously climbed on to its back.

Toot-toot! The horse began to move, forward and up and down. The steam organ had never stopped playing. Faster and faster the horses galloped but not too fast for a laughing girl to come scrambling up on to the platform and then on to the back of the horse three in front of where I was riding. I thought how pretty she was with her face all pink with excitement and her long, golden hair flowing. She was riding sidesaddle on a dapple grey horse, her frock and petticoat raised high enough to show the tops of her lace-up boots and give a hint of long, graceful legs.

The Lady Rowena, perhaps? But I knew her for Waggle's sister, Effie. I tried not to notice that a tall boy had climbed on to the horse beside her nor that he had stretched out an arm and laid a hand on her shoulder. It was Lanky and she was laughing into his eyes.

Leatherfaced men and women were lighting the naptha flares on the stalls as I set out for Washbrook. Folks were swarming in Newput High Street like tadpoles in a pond at hatching time but making much more sound. Stallholders were shouting their patter, the organ of Thurston's Galloping Horses still churning out the same tunes. In front of *The Dolphin*, a man was standing, swaying on his feet as he looked upwards at the swishing swingboats with their shouting boys and screaming girls. He was muttering that they would all be sick if they went any higher, a thought perhaps prompted by his own beer-bloated state.

There were still three pennies in my pocket. Never mind, I thought, they could be saved towards the cost of another book. Real darkness would not fall on this midsummer's day until later. Just now the world was wrapped in a soft warmth as in a half-wakening dream. As, alone, I crossed the North Bridges, I stopped in one of the recesses and looked over the parapet at the moving waters of the Ouse. A bat flitted above my head and, being young enough, I could hear its squeak. Beneath me, a fish rose to a fly and there was light enough from houses on the river bank to give a flickering gleam to the rippling circles that were left.

Farther on, I had to duck my head to avoid being struck in the face by a drowsy, droning dumbledor beetle. Under that young oak near the pair of cottages, a small swarm of cockchafers still circled.

I did not turn round when I heard the swish of bicycle tyres and the creaking of an unoiled chain. For I recognized the laughter of one of the two riders but not the voice of the one who was complaining that the leader was pedalling too bloody fast.

The laughing one was Totsie Varley and, as she rode past, she turned her head and called out "good night, Jacky Lloyd!" I felt myself blushing in the darkness. I hated being called "Jacky," it made me feel such a little boy, though I was glad she had spoken. Her companion, pedalling furiously, and panting like an asthmatic pump as he tried to keep pace with her, had no breath to speak to me, even had he wanted to do so. Dim as the light now was, I recognised the narrow shoulders and the weak profile as those of one of the "gents" as the boys of Newput called the young fellows who were at the cramming establishment.

I had been to Long Fair. There would be a second fair day tomorrow, but I didn't think I would bother to go.

CHAPTER NINETEEN

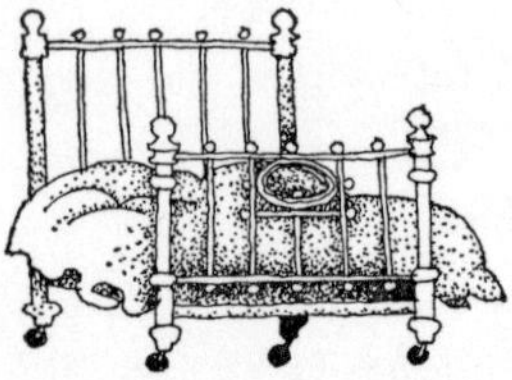

AGGIE'S HUSBAND

CHUCK TURNEY MARRIED his Aggie one Saturday morning between haytime and harvest. Bert Fowler gave him the morning off as well as strict orders not to be late at Hill Farm on Monday. Much to the disgust of Evan Hughes, they were married in Church, something Chuck had insisted on, he having sung in the choir as a boy.

Parson Blossomville had no other weddings on that day and, this being out of the beagling season, he made a proper job of it with a sermon on the text "love ye one another." Aggie wore a freshly washed and ironed dress that she had bought off the secondhand stall in Newput market and a veil made by her mother for her own wedding with much clicking of bobbins on a lace-pillow.

As they came out of the church, Mrs Rudd, a small child's grubby paw in either hand, whispered rather loudly that the roses Aggie was clutching as if they were a besom, came out of the Grange garden. She knew because her old man did a bit of work sometimes for Colonel Cobley. "Nobody else grows any like them!"

Sal Heffer threw two handfuls of rice and Old Jinny said it was a wicked waste of good food. I had once heard Dad say that Sal's name should have been Sheep as she was like a Border Leicester ewe with her long, white face.

In fact, Cornelia Cobley, the teapot incident forgiven if not forgotten, had cut the roses herself and given them to Aggie with her warmest wishes. The rice thrown by Sal Heffer was some that had been spilled on the floor of Mrs Perry's shop and swept up. Sal, as keen as a ferret when it came to something for nothing, had been in the shop at the time and begged the soiled rice.

As the couple walked down the gravel path, between the long-forgotten, grassy graves, Old Jinny rested her gaunt arms on a moss-grown, lop-sided tombstone and rasped "Mark my words, that poor gal is going to rue this day! Never no good to nobody, was that Chuck Turney!"

If Chuck heard Jinny's pronouncement, he was not worried as he strode along with Aggie's hand on his powerful arm. His Viking face was shining from a recent scrubbing, his black suit smelled faintly of mothballs and there was a splash of white on the left shoulder where a solitary swallow had wished him luck while Parson Blossomville was giving the blessing.

The honeymoon was a short one. Chuck hired Ernie Spraggins's grey pony, Punch, with the market cart he so often drew, and took his bride to Bedford where it was market day. For a time they sauntered through the streets, Aggie gasping "coo!" and "cor! Look at that, Chuck!" when she saw marvellous things in shop windows.

Aggie tried to interest her man in the statue of John Bunyan standing near St. Peter's church. She wondered what book John was reading but thought it must be something good, he was keeping the place so carefully with one hand.

Chuck stared at the statue in silence, and then, taking a firm grip on his bride's arm, steered her into the smoke filled taproom of a dark little inn. There they stayed while he drank pint after pint of bitter beer. Aggie, used neither to tobacco smoke nor to alcohol, coughed and pulled a wry face over one small glass of port and lemon, a drink which, she had been told, was normally reserved for "the gentry." She wondered why, for she would much rather have had a cup of good, strong tea with plenty of sugar.

Aggie's thoughts were on Honeymoon Cottage, where they were to live and her dreams of heaven be realised. At about nine o'clock, Chuck's thoughts were running in a similar groove, uppermost among them being that big, double bedstead with its brass knobs. Chuck had picked it up cheap when he found it among a lot of junk in the yard at the back of Alfy Mullard's shop in Newput, and now it almost filled one of the two rooms in Honeymoon Cottage.

Fetching his hand down on Aggie's thigh in a blow that might have broken the limb of a frailer woman, Chuck set down his empty pot and bellowed for all to hear "Ha, my gal, there's things to be done tonight as will amaze you! Let's be getting back."

He brought Punch out of the stable at the back of the pub and shut him in, as they say in those parts, to the market cart. He hoisted Aggie aboard as if she had been a baby, clambered up beside her, gathered the reins, gave them a shake and growled "gittup there!"

Punch set off at a steady jog and when they were clear of Bedford town and heading for the ancient bridge at Bromham, Chuck held the gig whip aganist the spokes of the wheel and this produced a reverberating tattoo. Punch knew the signal having heard it often before. It meant that the driver was market merry and expected the pony to take him home without guidance. He quickened his pace.

Chuck laid his beery face on Aggie's shoulder, gave a loud snore and fell asleep, lulled by the jogging motion of the cart. He did not even hear his bride's protests that he would bring the pony down and break its knees or tip them over the coping of the bridge where they would be drownded.

A dreadful shadow of a thought flitted through Aggie's mind; could the vinegarish prophecies of Old Jinny have just a little truth in their gloomy promises? Was Chuck after all no better than he was painted by the gossips of the village?

They had been married for about three weeks when Cornelia Cobley noticed that Aggie came to work on Monday mornings red-eyed, and sometimes not only red. One morning she saw that her left eye was surrounded by a big, blue bruise.

Now, in spite of her social ambitions or perhaps partly because of them, Cornelia had a warm heart and she was genuinely interested in human beings. She professed to take an interest in anyone who worked for her or her husband and she decided to tackle Aggie about her obvious troubles. This interest was prompted, in the first place, by genuine kindheartedness and, if there was also a touch of curiosity for its own sake, who was to blame her for it? Who knew what spicy secrets of life among the lower orders might not be revealed to her?

Aggie was polishing the leg of an up-ended chair, a reproduction Chippendale, sniffing away and rubbing at the turned wood as if it had done her a personal injury.

Cornelia cleared her throat loudly, but Aggie went on sniffing and polishing and did not look up. "Agatha!" said Cornelia "I would like a word with you."

"Yes, ma'am," stopping her work at last and standing upright. She gave a loud sniff and removed a dewdrop from her nose with the back of her hand. "Yes, ma'am."

"Have you something on your mind, Agatha, something that is worrying you?"

"N-no, nothing at all, I'm sure, ma'am." but Aggie's eyes were filling with tears and her upper lip was trembling. For the first time since she was a child, this seemingly hard woman began to weep. She wept silently, standing as straight as a telegraph pole while the tears trickled down the furrows of her cheeks until she wiped them away with the duster.

Cornelia went to her and, reaching upwards, put an arm across her shoulders. "Sit down, Aggie," she said softly. Gone now was the social nonsense; they were two women together and one of them was in trouble. "Sit down and tell me all about it, my dear."

Sitting now on one of the chairs she had polished with so much care, Aggie slumped forward, elbows on knees and screwed the duster between her hands. "It's my Chuck" she sobbed out. "Comes 'ome drunk on a Saturday night and knocks me about something dreadful, he does." A flood of tears followed and then she blurted "and I thought we were go-going to be so h-happy! I never expected married life to be like this!"

Cornelia did some hard thinking as she sat on another chair which she had drawn up beside Aggie. She patted her hands and murmured "There, there" while seeking a solution in her own mind. It would never do to suggest that Aggie should go to Long Bob; that would end any chance there was now of retrieving her dreams of bliss. She thought of Parson Blossomville but it occurred to Cornelia that Aggie, not being a member of his flock, would be shy of him.

What about that kindly but sanctimonious man, Evan Hughes? She quickly dismissed him, telling herself that he would only add to the unfortunate woman's misery by preaching at her and anger her by calling down the wrath of Heaven upon Chuck. Then, suddenly, she had an inspiration.

"Aggie!" cried Cornelia with unexpected familiarity and clasping her hands together. "Aggie, I have it! Just you go along and see Mrs Varley; they tell me she knows how to deal with men."

"What, *me*, ma'am? Me go into that 'ouse of shame?" A shudder vibrated Aggie's lean frame.

Cornelia smiled and squeezed the other's hand. "You've been listening to Mr Hughes, Aggie!" she said "Say what you like about the woman, but I am sure Mrs Varley would tell you exactly what to do. Just you ask her!"

The menfolk were all out on the farms except those few who, in obedience to a distant steam whistle, cycled to the dreary "works" six miles away. Their wives were busy, as wives always are, at those activities which are women's province and the children were all at school. Behind the Hilbury Heights the thunderheads were building up in a sky that was red with anger and an oppressive heat brought clouds of small flies—thunder flies we called them.

Even on this sultry summer afternoon, Aggie chose to wrap a shawl over her head and hunched shoulders as she turned into

Blackthorn Lane after first looking to left and right to make sure she was not seen. As Chuck, in their courting days, had told her, she moved like a longdog and she was soon striding up the path that led to the door of *The Lilacs*.

Two hours later, Aggie came out of *The Lilacs* and she did not bother to put the shawl over her head. Instead, she swung the coloured, patchwork length of knitting as if it had been a banner. There was a look on her creased face that came near to being a smile; determination, too.

What advice Dolly Varley had given to Aggie nobody but those two knew until Monday, but Aggie *did* tell her mother something else and her mother told everybody she met if they could find time to listen to her news. Totsie Varley was expecting.

When Poor Arry heard this surprising piece of news as he contemplated a broken gate, pig-poking stick over his arm, he blinked his watery eyes and said "It's lodged at last then, seem'ly." One of his lean cows turned her head and went on chewing the cud.

My father brought the news home after taking his mid-day pint of Mrs Pawsey's beer. "Missis," he boomed, grinning across the kitchen table, "Ernie Spraggins says Totsie is going to have a kid!"

"Nonsense! If anybody knows better than to go and do a silly thing like that, it's Totsie. Anyhow, how does Ernie Spraggins know?"

"The tale came first from Mrs Lute and then Ernie saw the gal in the *Red Lion*. If anybody knows a thing or two about breeding, it's Ernie. He says he could tell by the way she sat down. She was in the saloon bar and guess who was with her?"

"Could be one of a score, I should think. Though, come to think of it, I don't know many who would be seen for long in public with her. Who was it?" Ma went on ladling new potatoes out of an iron saucepan straight on to our waiting plates.

"That dopey son of Lord Somebody-or-other who is at the crammer's. Came out with the beagles once last season. Couldn't keep his eyes off Mary Blossomville then, until a hare got up. Then

Mary ran close to hounds as she always does and this lad collapsed in a ditch and had to be helped back to the pub. *You've* seen him. Got no chin!"

"Well, he must make up for it somewhere else!" Ma said as we sat down to our meal in the little kitchen that had once been a baker's oven.

We were good trenchermen, all three of us had real appetites and Ma enjoyed cooking for those who appreciated proper grub. We tucked into the food while that old and favoured one-eyed beagle, Dancer, sat underneath the table with the big tabby cat, Kit, who was purring in anticipation. Both knew that when we had finished with our plates they would be given them to lick.

Dad set down his plate on the tiles and watched with pleasure as the two animals licked the china till it shone. Then they waited for Ma to do the same with hers. They had a longer wait for mine. Though a healthy boy, I was an uncommonly slow eater.

"Another thing," Dad said "Ernie told me the young fool is going to marry her."

"But she's a tart!" Ma exclaimed.

"What about it?" Dad wanted to know, as Ma reached across the oven and brought out a rice pudding with the proper bay leaf and some nutmeg on its brown, top skin. "Totsie won't be the first strumpet to marry into the peerage." I made a mental note of another new word.

Aggie Turney, as she now was, may have leaked the news about Totsie, but the advice she received from Dolly Varley on how to deal with her own husband, Chuck, she kept to herself until she had acted upon it and then Cornelia Cobley was the first to hear about the results.

Cornelia sailed into her drawing room on a wave of Parma violet. She was fresh from her bath, a massive tin affair that had to be carried into her bedroom. She found Aggie flicking the mantelpiece with a feather duster in a carefree way that endangered the two china dogs and the imitation Ming horse. Cornelia would have protested if the danger to the ornaments had not been driven out of her head by the realization that Aggie was singing to herself.

The tune, though plainly that of a hymn, was a new one to Cornelia, for she had never heard it in church and she was sure the words were not in Hymns Ancient and Modern. They were something about only being an armour bearer.

Aggie, who had not noticed Cornelia's entrance, or if she had, gave no sign of having done so, went on with her dusting. Leaving the china dogs and horse, she transferred her attentions to others on canvas and began dusting the gilt that framed a picture of hounds and horses careering across what appeared to be a very dangerous stretch of countryside. There were terrible falls all over the place and nobody seemed to be taking the slightest notice of them.

"I have been giving a great deal of thought to your problem, Agatha."

So it was Agatha again, was it?

"What problem, ma'am?" Aggie stopped dusting and held the butt end of the duster against her sharp hip as daintily as a whipper-in would his hunting crop.

"Why, that matter we talked over together. About your husband beating you and so on."

"Oh, *that*!" the lines deepened from Aggie's jaws to her cheekbones. "I don't get none of that now."

"I am *so* glad, Aggie!" Aggie again now, it seems. "Tell me just what happened."

"Well, ma'am, I did what you said. I went to see Dolly Varley. Real helpful she was. O' course, she should know, having buried one and got another as isn't much good on her hands now."

"Yes, but what advice did Mrs Varley give you?"

Aggie straightened her long back and Cornelia could see she was nearly as tall as Chuck when she did that. "She said to me 'Don't you wait for him to start anything, my gal' she said 'you start on him first.' Quite understanding like, she was."

Like a barge coming to rest on a mud berth as the tide ebbs,

Cornelia sank her broad stern into a deep armchair. Eager to hear more, she asked "And *did* you start on him first?"

"I did and all, ma'am! When I heard my Chuck coming along the street, hollering and shouting and a-cursing and a-swearing, I says to myself 'Aggie, my gal, he's drunk!' and then I did just what Dolly had told me to do. I picks up the biggest saucepan I could lay my hands on and I waits behind the door."

"Do go on, Aggie!"

"Yes, and go on I did too. He comes stumbling through the doorway, bawling for me, but before he sees me, I ups with the saucepan and hits him over the head with it. Down he goes like a cartload of wuzzels and with just about as much sense in him and then I drops the pan, turns him on his back, kneels on his chest and gives him a proper pummelling."

"Well done you, Aggie!" Cornelia's admiration for the plucky woman overcame her gentility. "But what did your husband do?"

Aggie was resting one elbow on the mantelpiece now. "When he came round, he got up and went to the table without a word. I took his supper out of the oven—a bloater it was. My Chuck couldn't abide bloaters before, but he ate that one up, tail and bones and head and all and said it was bootiful. I've never had no more trouble with him and I wouldn't be married to nobody else in the world but my Chuck, not even to the son of a Lord!"

CHAPTER TWENTY

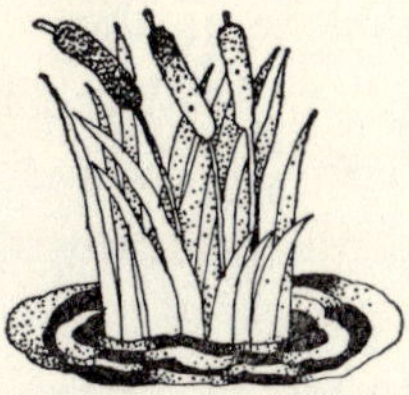

THE RIVER

FREDDY SAID NOT to tell his mum we were going down to the river. She had catched him a clout when he had mentioned something about doing this once before. People fell into rivers and got themselves drownded like that poor old chap when she was a gal. That's why that deep pool near the island was called Dead Man's Pit. So Freddy's mum mustn't be told. Like many other folk who lived far inland, the Rudds had a horror of water comparable with that which they felt towards the night air, against which all windows must be tightly shut.

No, said Eric, we wouldn't tell Freddy's mum where we were going. Another thing, we would set off by way of Gun Lane and then it would look as if we were going to Elverton Woods. Pushing his hands into his pockets and whistling *The Minstrel Boy*, he started walking. I was stepping out after him when Freddy stopped and looked round. "Go home, our Alby!" he said.

"Shan't!" said Alby, who had appeared from behind a garden hedge.

"If you don't go back, I'll ding you one!"

"No, you won't!"

"Yes I will!"

Freddy took three steps back and scuffled his feet, raising small puffs of dust from the dry surface of the road.

"If you don't take me with you I'll tell our mum you're going to the river!"

The sharp-witted Eric, who had taken in the situation, stopped whistling and said "I suppose the little beggar will have to come with us." He regarded Alby with open distate, as if he had been one of those fat, grey slugs found under stones. "All right, Alby, but it'll be no use bawling if you fall in, and wipe the snot off your nose!"

Like woods and spinneys, the river had to be approached with caution. True, the mowing grass had been cut, made into hay and carried; there was no longer a risk of trampling that down and making things difficult for the mowing machine. Already the lattermath was growing among the prickly stumps where the first crop had been cut.

On Long Meadow a herd of shorthorn bullocks grazed or chewed the cud. Fred Fowler had wintered them on higher ground and now they were waxing fat on pasturage enriched by the alluvial deposits of last February's floods. He wouldn't welcome a gang of boys upsetting his cattle. We moved in single file close beside a thick, thorn hedge, Eric leading, Alby in the rear.

Ahead, where the river swept round in a wide curve, I saw a silver glint and my nostrils picked up the scents of mud baking in the sun, of dead waterweeds and the tang of catmint. The nearness of water always excited me. I was for openly running to the bank but Eric motioned with his hand and made hushing sounds. We crept forward.

A tall alder leaned over the water, shaking blunt leaves and ruddy flowers in the light breeze. But there was no reflection in the dark pool of Dead Man's Pit. The island beyond was a jungle of reeds and nettles, of fragrant meadowsweet, flowering rush and catmint above which rose clumps of sallows.

A moorhen clucked as she poked out her head with its yellow bill and red knob. She did not see us hidden from her by a thick bed of bullrushes as she zigzagged between the dishlike leaves and yellow flowers of the waterbubbles. She spread her white tail feathers, perhaps as a safety signal to the flotilla of fluffy black chicks that swam behind her.

"Our Tod says you can eat moorhens," remarked Freddy.

"Yes," Eric agreed, "but there ain't much meat on them and they can't be plucked. You have to skin them."

Freddy stiffened and assumed his "pointer" pose. He held up a hand as if it were a forepaw. We too heard the splash of water and the sound of laughter. Alby opened his mouth but Eric put a hand over it, at the same time whispering "Come on!" He led the way, crouching low, along the river bank in the direction of the sounds.

The tall vegetation of the water's edge and the clumps of bull-rushes ended abruptly at a shallow place where the bank was gently shelving so that the cattle could go down to drink. I noticed first the piles of clothes on the bank, the flowery frocks, the petticoats with their lace edges, the cotton stockings and the lace-up boots. Then I looked towards the river itself, sparkling over the stony shallows. There, with the water rippling round their legs, were three young girls.

They were Down End girls and, when they saw us, the two smaller ones giggled, one sticking a finger into her mouth. The third, who was an inch or two taller, must have become suddenly conscious of the approach of puberty, for she put her hands together between her legs. She reminded me of a picture that hung in Granny Bunting's drawing room. What did my father call it? Pre-Raphaelite, was it?

Living as I did in an artist's household, the un-clothed female figure was no mystery to me, any more than I supposed it was to these other boys who lived with sisters in very cramped quarters.

To show his unconcern, Eric began whistling but stopped for long enough to give a jerk of his head as a signal to move on. We followed him along the river bank. Glancing back at Freddy, I was surprised to see a shocked look on his face. Alby was trotting along four yards behind, making strange, crooning noises.

"Our Dad says as if Our Nellie shows her ha'penny to the boys when she gets older, he'll smack her bum." remarked Freddy.

I was thinking about those three nude girls. My Lady Rowena, I told myself, was not one of them. She had to be somebody different from all the rest.

The flies, the plague of all rivers, were worrying Fred Fowler's bullocks. We sat on the bank and watched them as they stuck their tails in the air as if to outdo the bullrushes then sprang off the ground, all four feet together, and made short charges.

"Got the gad," remarked Eric. He broke off a long, coarse grass and chewed it. Freddy stared straight in front of him at the water. We had forgotten Alby until we heard a splash and a gurgling yell.

"He's fell in!" shouted Freddy, scrambling to his feet

It was true. Alby must have leaned too far over a deep pool and lost his balance. We ran to the bank in time to see his urchin face break surface. A slimy length of dark green waterweed was round his neck.

"Tread water, Alby!" I shouted, but I might as well have advised him to fly. With another gurgle, his head went underwater again. But the ever resourceful Eric had climbed out on the limb of a willow and, reaching down, managed to grab a skinny arm. Between us, we hauled him out. Alby sprawled on the grass while the water ran out of his sodden clothes and the bullocks stopped their gadding to come and watch us, lowering their heads and snorting.

It was all our fault, according to Alby, and when he told Our Mum, we wouldn't half cop it! Freddy said he had told him not to come, but he looked worried as he said so. Eric told Alby to stop bawling and take his clothes off; they could be nearly dry by the time we set off for home.

Alby's teeth were chattering and he was shivering so violently that Freddy had to help him undress. As his last, nondescript garment was pulled over his head, I could not help staring. His skin was so white that I wondered whether this was the first time it had ever been exposed to the fresh air, except his feet which were so black that I thought that, until today, they could not have known water for a very long time.

After all, there was no such luxury as a bathroom in the whole village. It was said that even Old Billy and Parson Blossomville made use of a peculiar vessel called a hip-bath. We ourselves made a regular habit of filling the copper with rainwater from the butt and heating it. As Ma said, this was a change from brewing wine. Then we would take down the big, tin washing tray from its nail and, if weather was cold, set it in front of the kitchen stove. In warm weather, the bath was put in the barn which made a shorter carry for the hot water from the copper.

Eric said Alby ought to run round the field to warm himself up and Freddy thought this a good idea. He could put his boots on to save his feet from the thistles. Between us, we pulled the little chap to his feet and gave him a push as a start.

Alby started slowly at first, sobbing as he stumbled over the grass, then, as he grew warmer, he appeared actually to be enjoying himself. Round the edge of the field he went, at a shambling run, the herd of bullocks snorting and skipping after him.

Alby stopped running and, as he stood there, panting, he started to laugh. The bullocks stuck hooves out in front of them and this brought them to a sudden halt. One let out a bellow and another, bolder than the rest, took three paces forward, dropped its head and thrust a warm, moist muzzle against Alby's skinny, white bottom. The boy lurched forward, and for a moment, I thought he was going to fall on his face. Instead, he recovered his balance and, laughing loudly now, turned round.

He waved his arms, he shouted a piping "*how-how-how*," that imitation of a dog's bark which never fails to get cattle moving. The herd swung round as if they had been polo ponies and, heads and tails up, set off across the field.

Yelling with delight, Alby ran after them. With those hard boots, passed down from older brothers, unlaced on his feet, it was a shambling gait, but carried the boy along at a surprising pace until he stepped on the end of one leather bootlace. This brought him down, full sprawl, in a fresh cowpat, but it did nothing to detract from his enjoyment. Getting up again, he ran on after the stampeding herd, still "*how-howing*."

We three elder boys stood and stared in horrified silence. Whilst we looked upon wild creatures, if edible, as fair game, farm stock was something sacred. Interfering with it in any way was one of the greatest crimes of the countryside. And here was little Alby running bullocks that should have been fattening themselves. We were so intent upon watching the committing of this crime that we did not see a man ride a roan cob up to the gate at the farther side of the field. The first we knew about this was when we heard Fred Fowler, for he it was, roar "Hi, you blasted young whippersnapper, what the hell do you think you're doing?"

Leaning out of the saddle, Fred opened the gate, rode the cob through and closed it behind him. Then he put the cob into a canter and, brandishing an ashplant stick, headed towards Alby. "I'll tan the hide off you, you little varmint!" he shouted.

Alby ran really fast now, sometimes turning a frightened face as he looked at his pursuer. Again he tripped but, howling now, recovered and ran on.

Fred Fowler took no notice of us as he rode by, but I noticed that he was grinning and that he had slowed the cob to a trot. I had an idea Fred was enjoying himself, for he was noted for a peculiar sense of humour.

In a corner of the field there was a second gate with the start of a lane beyond it. Alby headed for this and, reaching it, clambered over and was in the lane. This gave the boy a fair lead.

We three walked quickly behind, ready to bolt should the farmer turn his rage upon us. We could hear Alby howling his way up the lane. We gathered the rest of the story when we reached the village; there were plenty willing to tell us how the boy ran through Down End and past Honeymoon Cottage. Luckily, for his own peace of mind, Evan Hughes was not looking out of the wheelwright's shop, and Jinny was not at the pump.

Behind Alby, at a jog which was fast enough to keep the lad

moving without actually being overtaken, rode Fred Fowler. But the farmer reined in before he reached Up End. Afterwards, he said he knew too much from his experience with animals to face Mother Rudd when she saw her youngest son in the village street. And he, as Fred put it, dressed only in a layer of cowshit and a pair of big boots.

Eric, Freddy and I too, knew better than to enter the village at once. We would have been blamed for not looking after Alby properly. And why hadn't we brought his clothes with us? Freddy got the customary "ding" for not doing so when, eventually, he went home. His big sister, Rosie, who was in service at the Rectory, had been sent down to Long Meadow to fetch Alby's clothes. The bullocks had tossed them all over the place, too, and one had put a horn through the shirt.

CHAPTER TWENTYONE

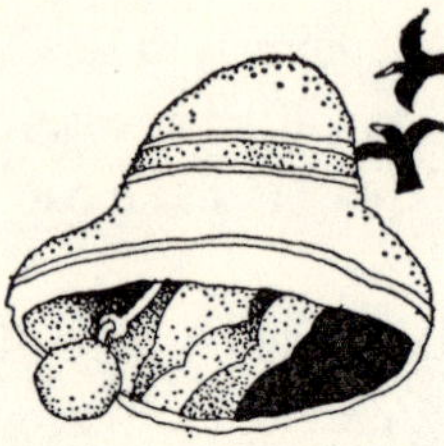

THE CHIMNEY

EVERY DAY EXCEPT Sunday, the One O'clock Bell was rung from the square tower of the Norman church. This was to tell the menfolk, at their work in the fields, that bavor time had come. Stumper, Turnips his brother, Chuck Turney and the rest of them then laid down scythes, fagging-hooks or whatever other implements they had been using, or growled "whoa there" to their teams. Fred Fowler, who was a bit hard of hearing, knew when the One O'clock Bell rang because Blossom, his chestnut mare, at once lay down, whether she was in harness or out of it.

They put down any sharp instruments with care, to preserve the keenness of the blade and for the sake of safety. If they had been working with horses, then they took nosebags and hung them by leather straps about the sweaty necks and watched as velvety muzzles snorted and snuffled at the mixture of chaff and oats.

In wet weather, they threw sacks over the backs of the horses and, tucking the corners of other sacks into each other, made hoods to protect their own heads and shoulders from the rain.

Then, settling themselves under the shelter of a hedgerow, putting their feet in the ditch, they opened big bags made of plaited rushes. They would bring out their "bavor" with the calculated, deliberate movements of the farm labourer, movements that townsmen find so irritating in their slowness—until they try to keep pace with them.

Cold, fatty, boiled bacon, bread plastered thickly with pork dripping, a huge clanger or, maybe, half a cottage loaf and a great hunk of leathery cheese to be cut with a singlebladed shut-knife which was used for castrating lambs and piglets.

After he had munched his fill, any remains were stowed back in the basket, lips wiped on the back of a soiled hand and a quart bottle taken out. The screw stopper was removed with a twist of a powerful wrist, the bottle tipped to the mouth and a contented glugging came from a dry throat. Nearly always, the contents of the bottle was cold tea.

As Church sexton, it was Stumper's duty to see that the One O'clock Bell's note should be heard across field and woodland and riverside meadow every weekday but, since his daily work kept him out in those fields himself, his wife deputised for him.

Mrs Stumper was a fine figure of a woman with hair of that fair tint which the years spare for so long. She and Stumper lived in the Blue Cottage, one of the four owned by my father, and they paid eighteen pence a week in rent. Three of the cottages drew drinking water from the same well. Water for washing purposes came, rather green and slimy, from the big barrel which each cottage had to catch rain water from barn roofs, the only ones not covered by thatch.

Nobody complained if the bell did not ring exactly at one o'clock according to Greenwich; country time is governed by the needs of animals as the seasons are by crops, so little store is set by clocks. Besides, it might be that Mrs Stumper had been busy at the precise hour. She might have been getting in her washing, feeding the hens or pigs, or cleaning the inside of the Blue Cottage. She was a great scrubber and duster was Mrs Stumper and her husband was devoted to her in a quiet, undemonstrative way. He had been heard to boast, over a pint of Mrs Pawsey's beer, that he could eat his meals off the floor—if he was so minded, which he never was. After his second pint, Stumper said that his wife had yet another virtue; she was of the right build to keep a man warm o' nights.

On this particular day, Mrs Stumper tucked her white apron up around her waist and went bustling off towards the church at what may have been ten minutes to one. Afterwards, Sal Heffer, who had been watching from behind the lace curtains of her diamond-paned front window, said she could see by the way she was swinging her hips that Mrs Stumper was in a hurry.

The air inside the church was cool and the sunlight slanted steeply down through the windows of one side, bearing on its shafts the colours of the solemn faced saints and showing up the dust on the pews. Mrs Stumper paused in the middle of the centre aisle for a moment to recover her breath. This done, she made a token obeisance to the altar before going to a single bellrope with its gaily coloured, woollen handgrip. As the first resonant *dong* pealed out, a pair of nesting jackdaws flew from a slit in the tower, a slit which we boys knew had been built in the masonry to enable an archer to aim his arrow at the right target.

The jackdaws wheeled round the grinning gargoyles then, yacking away, they circled higher and higher. They had heard that bell for many a month but they always responded to its sound.

Dong! As if the bell exalted in its single bass note ringing out in triumph over the silence of its four companions.

Dong! Legend has it that all five bells were cast at a foundry in Washbrook itself, a foundry of which, if it ever existed, no trace remains.

Dong! The note burst on the summer air and floated over the village, out across green pastures and fields of corn that were now showing a hint of their golden future. As the note faded, its place was taken by a vibrating hum, making the eardrums tingle.

The bell was supposed to be rung for five minutes but, the clock face being, naturally, on the outside of the church tower and Mrs Stumper not carrying a watch, the timing was left to the judgement of the ringer. On this day, the bell rang for exactly three and a half minutes. Mrs Heffer said so, she having timed the ringing by the big clock on her kitchen shelf. But then, she was always a nosy body and folks said the late William Heffer was a lucky man to have quit her side for another world when he did.

Mrs Stumper clattered down the aisle, out of the open door and bustled through Up End on her way back to the Blue Cottage. Inside once more, she spread a white damask cloth on the deal table in the only downstairs room and set out fork, knife and a plate. A cottage loaf with its top storey slightly lopsided and standing on a breadboard was put beside them. Then a glance in the cupboard, built to fit the corner where it stood, just to assure herself that the cold bacon and cheese were still there.

Taking a zinc bowl with a wooden handle to it, Mrs Stumper scooped water from the butt outside the backdoor and set it down on the bench in the little barn. A much-used slab of yellow soap rested on a cracked saucer and, after she had lathered a flannel, she scrubbed her cheeks until they shone.

For Mrs Stumper was going to visit her married daughter who lived at Hilbury. She was taking flowers and peas picked from their own garden, and the evenings being long, she need not come back to the Blue Cottage till quite late.

Stumper did not hurry home after his work was done; he had no reason to when his wife would not be there and when he knew his meal was a cold one. He went first to *The Dog and Duck* to slake a proper summer thirst with Mrs Pawsey's beer. And there he met his younger brother, Turnips.

The beer was drawn from a barrel, one of a row standing on a stone shelf in a cool, dark room known as the cellar because the floor was two steps below that of the tavern. Mrs Pawsey, a capable, square-built widow who had worn black ever since Pawsey died ten years ago, brought the beer in thick, china mugs.

The brothers were dressed alike, except for their neckcloths, Stumper's being red spotted with blue and Turnip's blue with red spots. They had striped flannel shirts with brown, unbuttoned weskits over them, no jackets, and corduroy trousers. Lengths of bagstring were tied below their knees to keep the trousers loose over those joints and to prevent any critturs from crawling up inside.

Their nailed boots were bullnosed and unyielding as iron.

The two had been close together as boys but, later on, Turnips took it into his head to go for a soldier. Some said he had got a girl into trouble, but Turnips couldn't hear them for he was in all the din of helping to relieve Mafeking. Now, living almost within spitting distance of each other, they were close in spirit again as well as dwellings. If one killed a pig, then his wife would take a plate of fry or chitterlings over to the other's cottage and if one had more runner beans than he could use, then a dishful was handed over.

So they had little need for words between each other except absolutely essential ones. However, on the evening when Mrs Stumper had gone off to see her married daughter at Hilbury, Stumper had something important to tell his brother. They had started on their second pints when he mentioned it.

"I'd like to give the missis a proper treat when she comes back from Hilbury." Stumper was watching Turnips out of his grey eyes over the blue rim of his pot. He needed help in his scheme.

"Ah." Turnips grunted and interested himself once more in his beer.

"Sort of surprise her when she gets home."

Turnips set down his pot and tugged at his moustache which some would have described as a "heavy military." "*Surprise your missis*? Take a bit o' doing, won't it?"

"It's something that's been on my mind for a couple of years now."

"Ah." Turnips picked up his pot again. "Well, what is this surprise treat?"

"I'd like to sweep the chimney before she comes back."

"*Sweep the chimney, man*? Why where would you get the brushes? There's none that I knows of nearer than Newput, and they belong to Sooty Smith. He'd never lend them to you, knowing it would be doing himself out of a job!"

"Don't want no brushes. But I *do* want somebody to help—steady the ladder and that sort of thing." Now Stumper was looking at Turnips in a way which elder brothers have.

Turnips shifted his feet and took a long pull at his beer. "Oh, well, I daresay I could manage that—if that's all you want."

Stumper had already finished his own beer and he got up from the high-backed settle, all six feet of him, like a fire-escape being raised. "Drink up, man! We've no time to lose."

Together with my parents I had a ringside seat, as you might say, at the sweeping of the Blue Cottage chimney, for two of our upstairs windows overlooked it.

The brothers came to the Blue Cottage carrying one of Ned Varley's ladders between them. Putting it up to the thatched roof needed a foot on the third rung, a pulling by one man and a hand-over-hand pushing by the other. This accomplished, with a lot of "to you" and "over a bit", they went off, Stumper into the cottage, Turnips along the path between the apple trees.

Stumper was first back and he was carrying a coiled clothes-line which he hung over a rung of the ladder while he grubbed about amongst broken forks and bottomless buckets until he unearthed a brick. He was tying this on one end of the line when Turnips came back along the path dragging a freshly uprooted gooseberry bush, the thorns of which made no impression on the tough skin of his hands. He was holding the bush by its soil-covered roots and the leafy twigs raised clouds of dust as they swept along the ground.

The brothers must have worked out the whole operation before they started on it, but this is the way with countrymen who see little point in unplanned experimentation.

While Stumper finished tying the knot, Turnips made the bush fast to the other end of the line and their only comments were in the form of grunts and snorts. That is, until three young Rudds came clattering out of the back premises of their home which was next to the Blue Cottage.

Alby Rudd was enjoying a slice of bread as thick as a doorstep and covered with pork dripping, much of which was smeared across his cheeks. Freddy was industriously picking his nose and Our Nellie was sucking a finger which, owing to this habit, was less grubby than her other ones. On the faces of all three was that detached stare which their elders find so irritating when directed on them by the young.

As he tested the knot on the bush end of the clothes-line, Turnips looked round over his shoulder and observed the Rudds. "What do you want?" he asked. The Rudds continued to stare. "'Aven't you got nothing better to do than stand there?" Alby licked the last crumb of what he called "bup" from his finger and then explored his lips with his tongue. He still stared.

"Stand foot!" called out Stumper, gripping the sides of the ladder and beginning to climb. He did this rather lopsidedly, as one end of the clothesline was over a shoulder and the brick tucked under one arm.

Our Nellie took her finger out of her mouth but did not close her lips. "Cor!" she exclaimed as Stumper nearly dropped the brick and, in saving it from falling, caused the ladder to wobble. "'E nearly dropped it!" Nellie yelled delightedly and Turnips swung round and leaned his body against the ladder so that he was free to shake his fist. "Beggar off!" he growled.

"Shan't!" Our Nellie screeched, knowing that if Turnips took his foot off the ladder rung where it rested the ladder would slip. "'E's going to drop it, *'e's going to drop it*!"

"Never mind the snotty-nosed little varmints, keep your bloody foot on the ladder!" Stumper grumbled. By now, feeling his boot toes digging into the thatch between the rungs, he was easier in his mind and soon able, by bracing his knees against the ladder, to raise himself so that he could drop the brick down the chimney.

Even behind our own windows we could hear the clumping and banging as the brick went down and we watched, fascinated, as the clothesline whipped its way up to the roof and into the stone chimney. Afterwards, in telling the story, Stumper said that line nearly whipped his right ear off.

Stumper came down much faster than he had gone up and both he and Turnips went into the cottage. We heard Stumper say "Pull, man, pull!" and more "Cors" from Our Nellie as the clothesline, which had gone slack as soon as the brick touched bottom, tautened once more. Up the sloping roof went that huge gooseberry bush; it was jerked to the coping of the chimney top and there paused as if it had taken root.

"Pull, Turnips, *pull man, pull!*"

The bush quivered as if afflicted with an ague and then, slowly folding its thorny branches as if they were the struts of an umbrella, resigned itself to its fate and disappeared down the square chimney.

A great silence lay over Up End. I could hear the ticking of our grandfather clock and the purring of Kit from where he lay sprawled on a windowsill. The beagles were quiet in their kennels across the yard. Even the Rudds were silent, and Our Nellie had her finger in her mouth again. I thought of the lull before the great battles of history with the ranks drawn up facing each other and waiting for the first shot to be fired.

Slowly, the door of the Blue Cottage opened and a great, black cloud of soot billowed out. The Rudds scuttled off to those complicated wooden buildings that housed fowls and rabbits and pigs behind their home.

Out of the black cloud came the sound of coughing, hacking and spitting, and then we saw the whites of two eyes as Turnips rubbed the smarting lids open. He was followed by Stumper, also rubbing his eyes, and I was reminded of the troupe of nigger minstrels which I had once seen on a rare trip to the seaside.

When Stumper had stopped coughing, he said "Come and give your face a dabble in the water butt and then we'll go and wash this soot out of our throats with a drop of Mrs Pawsey's beer!"

Both men disappeared behind the Blue Cottage, and when they reappeared, they were drying their faces on the ends of their neckcloths. They went clumping off in the direction of *The Dog and Duck* and I heard Stumper say to his brother "Well, Turnips me boy, we swept the bloody chimney."

Not long after the brothers had gone, leaving Ned Varley's ladder still leaning against the thatch of the Blue Cottage, Mrs Stumper came back. She had walked by way of the footpath that runs close by the side of Thickthorn Wood and she was thinking of all the family news she had to tell Stumper. He was sure to be in a good mood for listening after his supper of cold bacon and cheese. She was glad she had looked out a nice, clean cloth for the table; it would be something to make up for her not being there herself to give him his food.

Nobody saw Mrs Stumper when she went inside the Blue Cottage, but all of us in Up End heard her when she came out again. Folks said it took Stumper three months to live it down and that he had a terrible task in persuading Mrs Stumper to go on ringing the One O'clock Bell. At first she said that them as thought themselves clever enough to sweep chimneys could ring blooming bells too.

CHAPTER TWENTYTWO

Camping

IN SPITE OF Freddy's comments on the effects of too much reading, I had been taking in another book. This one was called *Scouting for Boys* and there was a lot in it about the joys of living out of doors. The book had been written by a man who had done this sort of thing in many wild places. His name was Baden-Powell and he must have been one of those happy men who are able to enter into the mind of a boy and see the world through his eyes, as were Kipling and Masefield.

The more I thought about this camping the more attractive it became. I kept the idea to myself until I saw the scrap of rick-sheet lying in a corner of Mrs Pyecroft's barn. This was when I went in there to look for a beagle who had strayed from the pack in the course of morning exercise, and in response to Dad's shout of "get round 'em, boy!"

That same evening, I told Eric and Freddy that we ought to go camping. My suggestion did not draw the enthusiasm I had hoped for "What, sleep out o' doors like the soldiers?" asked Eric. Freddy just ground a heel into the middle of a thistle. Then he said something about the damp ground and the night air. I found myself marvelling that these boys, who thought little of weathering any conditions while awake, had an inherent fear of sleeping under the night sky, even in summer.

When an idea had formed in my head, I seldom gave up until I had tried it out. The bee continued to buzz in my bonnet and if my two usual companions would not listen to its loud droning then I must find others who would. Pedro would come camping, that is, if Aunt Ede could be persuaded to let him. Here Ma could help by talking to her sister on the benefits boys could gain by looking after themselves in camp. I showed her the book. Ma said she didn't care about that but she would be delighted to have me and any of my disreputable chums out of her way for a couple of days. Yes, she would tackle Aunt Ede about Pedro's camping.

Aunt Ede wanted to know where we would be going and I chimed in that we would be camping in Cut-throat Spinney, beside the river. I had asked Fred Fowler and he had said it would be all right as long as we didn't chase his cattle like that young devil did last week. Aunt Ede wasn't interested in Fred Fowlers' cattle; it was the thought of that deep, wide river which disturbed her. "Ooh, our Flo," she exclaimed, putting a hand to her cheek, "do you mean they will be by the *water*?"

Ma said not to worry: thanks to the efforts of Old Bull, the schoolmaster, we both could swim. She had another thought. What were we going to do for a tent? Then I told them about Mrs Pyecroft's bit of rick-sheet and how she had said I could borrow it provided I didn't forget to take it back.

We planned our camping for the following week-end. Then Cousin Dick could come too as he would be staying with us. In that way, Ma said, she could have two young varmints out of her way at the same time. Dick's home was near enough to London for him to be looked upon in Washbrook as a Londoner, yet his natural tastes were those of a country boy. Indeed, as is the case with many town boys, he may have appreciated country life all the more because it was fresh to him.

Shanny lent us his handtruck to cart the ricksheet, three blankets, a frying-pan, a kettle and a few other necessities down to Cut-throat Spinney. Up End had never seen anything like it and those who watched us pulling the loaded truck did not make a single remark. Even Alby and Our Nellie were silent. In Down End, Jinny stopped her pumping to stare and the *clink-clink* ceased in the smithy. Tom Barnes had knocked a couple of bricks out of the wall so that he could take a squint at what was going on outside, when he felt like it.

Once again I had borrowed Ma's clothesline and, in the spinney, we strung this in a double length between a beech and an alder tree. Over this we slung the length of rickcloth and declared it to be a grand tent. Cousin Dick said it looked a bit on the short side but Pedro told him we could put our jackets over our feet if they stuck out at the end.

The next thing, I announced, was to look for a water supply. It said so in the book. We could hear the tinkle of water finding its way over the twenty rough yards to the river and were soon able to trace this to a spot where it came bubbling out of the ground amongst a cluster of small stones. A long time afterwards, I discovered this to be the result of a broken farm drain. At the time, we declared the water to be of the purest spring variety.

That evening, we swam in the river where it flows past Cutthroat Spinney. Pedro and Cousin Dick knew a bit about fishing and they had brought rods but, while they sat watching their floats, I wandered over the fields. I came back rejoicing with a double handful of mushrooms which I had found growing on the fringes of Fred Fowler's fragrant muckheap.

Pedro said it was a pity they had not caught a fish as then we could have eaten it with the mushrooms. As it was, we fried them, together with a pound of sausages, over a fire of sticks. We all agreed that this camping was a wonderful thing.

Sleep did not come easily. We lay awake listening to the rustling of rushes and the occasional *plop* as a water vole dived from the bank. An otter whistled and a nightingale trilled as a full moon floated up out of the mists of the river valley. Although we had scraped hollows for our hips, as it said in the book, the ground was still hard and, in spite of tucking our spare clothes round our toes, they grew colder as the night wore on.

"I wonder why this place is called Cut-throat Spinney," mused Dick, turning on his back and drawing his cold feet up under his body.

"Don't you know?" I said, and paused for long enough to be impressive before continuing. "Why, the police were after some chap who had done a murder and he came in here and slit his own throat."

"They say his ghost is here still," said Pedro, and there was a huskiness in his voice.

I knew what we were all thinking: that if this had been in the light of day we would have laughed at the idea of ghosts. Now, with the moon showing her hazy face through the river mists and the noises of the night around us, we were not so sure. We lay there, wide awake, and morning seemed a long way off.

A shriek shrilled out from the mist and I felt my backhair stand on end. I could hear my heart beating. The silence following the scream seemed to last for a very long time. It was broken by a low hissing that sounded overhead.

I crawled out of the cover of Mrs Pyecroft's ricksheet and looked upwards. There, perched on a low branch of the beech tree was a barn owl, so close that I actually saw its eyes blink before it flapped away, rather clumsily, on wide, blunt-ended wings.

Next morning as, with blankets wrapped about our shoulders, we sat around a small fire, eating bacon and eggs, nobody spoke of the joys of camping. Perhaps I hadn't read enough of the book before putting the ideas it outlined into practice.

We stuck our camping for another day and night and then, piling blankets, cooking pots, fishing rods and Mrs Pyecroft's ricksheet and all on Shanny's truck, we left Cut-throat Spinney.

In Up End, Eric and Freddy were standing by the lamp-post. "Wotcher!" Eric said, just as if we were not returning from a great adventure. Freddy kicked a stone and grinned. We were glad of an excuse to rest from pulling and pushing that rather heavy truck uphill.

"You didn't stay very long," Freddy said "I bet it was cold at night." We three adventurers insisted that it was nothing of the kind, but perhaps we insisted too much for Freddy grinned again. We strained at the truck once more, the other two making no move to help us.

That evening, there was a meeting of the Show Committee in the *Cobley Arms*, for the Down End pub was the handiest for the field—where the show was to be staged. As secretary, Dad, naturally, was at the meeting. But Ma was having a card party at home. The Nuss was one and old Miss Peacock, she who had been at the court of a German princess, so there was Scotch whisky on the table, at three shillings and sixpence a bottle. Another player was the wife of Harry the Intendance. When we went to the open window, we could see them all sitting round the table and listen to the chatter and laughter. There was always laughter when Mrs Harry was with them.

Pedro said he was not going home yet and Cousin Dick was staying with us, so we just stood about or sat on the garden wall. Our camp seemed a long way off already. As we spoke of it and recalled the happenings, we came to realise that we had enjoyed even the cold nights. There was another boy with us now. Danny had come along with his mother, Mrs Harry, but we knew why: he wanted to hear all about The Camp, not that he ever said so. He was one of those boys who could be talked into doing almost anything by being told he dare not.

There was that time we dared him to go into a field and face Pharaoh Bugbrooke's shorthorn bull with a hedge stake for a sword and a sack for a cloak. We others had watched from the other side of a gate. I was reckoned to be the fastest runner in Washbrook, next perhaps to Waggle, but neither of us could have outrun Danny on that day—nor have come over a gate as quickly.

In time, Eric and Freddy turned up, as I hoped they would. They did not mention camping but, somehow, an idea formed in my mind that they resented the presence of Danny. After all, he never came on our expeditions and he was from Down End. We all became surprisingly quiet for a gathering of boys.

We heard Mrs Harry, in her strong, clear voice, telling the other card players how Evan Hughes had denounced in chapel "certain houses" in the village. Over one in Blackthorn Lane, he could only shake his head and mutter something about a den of sin, but he was more specific about others in Up End. These he named as "gambling hells."

The idea that playing a game for halfpenny stakes constituted something like a mortal sin was so funny that Up End rang with their laughter. I could see Sal Heffer poking her head out of a window.

Eric started whistling *The Minstrel Boy* but he broke off when Danny announced that he was going to pee. I knew what that half smile meant on Eric's face and was not surprised when he said to Danny "bet you daren't do it out of a bedroom window."

"Bet I dare!"

"Do it then, out of that one!" Eric pointed to an upstairs window immediately above the one from which the female voices were coming.

Danny ran in through our front door and we heard his feet on the stairs. We all watched as we saw him open a casement and stick out his head. Before he could follow this with that part of his anatomy essential to the proposed operation, a gust of wind sprang up as unexpectedly as such gusts will in summer. The casement slammed and there was the tinkling sound of broken glass falling on to the path stones.

For a few moments there was complete silence. Even the chatter of the card players ceased. We boys stared, fascinated, at the window where Danny's head was sticking through a broken pane. There was a frozen look of surprise on his face. Then Ma put her head out of the window below, looked upwards and asked "What on earth are you doing there, Danny?" She followed the question with a peal of laughter.

Danny's mother, Mrs Harry, a handsome woman, as Ernie

Spraggins said, strode out of the front door and also looked upwards. She saw her son's head framed by a broken window and she addressed him as became the wife of a county official. Look what he had done to Mrs Lloyd's window. Think of her and poor Mr Lloyd lying in bed all night, shivering with cold. Just wait until Danny's father was told all about it! And what was he doing, putting his head out of the window, anyhow?

Danny blurted out that he only wanted to pee. He followed this statement with a loud bellow and went on howling too loudly for anyone to hear what more Mrs Harry had to say.

We other boys were shocked. Not by Danny's motive for putting his head out of the window, not by the fact that he had broken the glass with his head, but because he was actually *crying*.

Big boys didn't cry, unless they were like poor Kipper who had had the spirit beaten out of him. We felt that Danny had failed the brotherhood. We noticed, though, that when he set up this wailing, his mother stopped telling him off. After another minute or two, in fact, she was asking if he had hurt himself while she went inside and upstairs to comfort him.

A short while later, things were almost normal again, the card-playing resumed, the laughter and talk coming from the open window downstairs once more, the window upstairs closed. Ma had said nobody was to worry about the broken pane. It wasn't a big one anyway and Ned Varley would put a new one in for very little money.

Danny had rejoined us, but he had nothing to say, just looking at the ground, till Eric said, slowly and very quietly, "Danny, *you cried*!"

The boy from Down End brightened and even smiled. "I wasn't crying *really*," he said "but I knew if our Mum thought I was, then she wouldn't tell our Dad to give me a hiding."

So that was all right, we told ourselves. Danny hadn't cried at all, really. Then Freddy looked worried. "It might have been bad," he said. "You might have cut your winkle off!"

"And then," commented Eric, "you'd have been no more use to a gal than one of Fred Fowler's bullocks is to a cow."

THE BAND

THE WIDOW PYECROFT said we could have her Home Close for the show and might use the tithe barn as well. There wasn't much in the barn except empty sacks, a stack of wuzzel and the cutter. But the kids were not to play skittles with the wuzzels like they did when she lent the barn for a chapel tea.

Dad and the committee were as pleased as a dog with a street of lamp-posts. They could have the fruit and vegetables at one end of the barn, the children's flowers in the middle and the baby show at the other end—properly screened, of course, since the little mites would have to be undressed. Sacks would have to be thrown over the wuzzel-cutter to make sure nobody got cut. Mrs Pawsey promised to lend the trestle tables she kept for outdoor parties.

For all Ma's doubts about Pharaoh Bugbrooke's generosity, that farmer promised a pig to be well greased and raced for by the women-folk. It was a six months old Tamworth hog and so lean and hard that its backbone stuck up like a bristly ridge of rock. Pharaoh had grinned through his black whiskers when Dad tackled him about the pig.

"Where do you think a poor, hardworking farmer is going to get the money to make up the price of a pig?" he asked.

"Surely you've got one that wouldn't be missed. The runt of a litter perhaps. And think of the fun we'd all have in watching the race!"

After plucking his beard for a minute or two and humming and hahing, Pharaoh had said "We-ell, there is one you can have, now I come to think of it. Yes, I'll give a pig." Turning on his heel, he stumped away, using his ash stick as if it had been a third leg. For an idea had sprung up in the tangled mind of Pharaoh Bugbrooke as he remembered Cronje, one of a litter farrowed by a Tamworth sow called Marigold and himself named after the President of the Boers. The rest of the litter were all good doers that guzzled their swill and dutifully put on weight. Cronje ate more than his fair share of the swill, but, while he grew fast in length of leg, he did not fatten.

From the day he promised the pig until the one before the show, Pharaoh took to rising from his bed half-an-hour early—and he was always up at first light. Then he would take the border collie sheep-dog and the lurcher bitch and tell them to chase Cronje round and round the orchard until all three had had enough.

The dogs meant no harm to the pig and the pig knew it: all looked upon the exercise as a game, but after a few weeks of this treatment, Cronje could run almost as fast as the lurcher. Pharaoh laughed quietly as he thought of possible contestants in the race and their chances of catching the pig. He did this with some relish, congratulating himself upon his knowledge of the anatomical details of some of them.

My father wanted to parade his beagles round the show ring in the interval but Ma put the damper on that by saying "Don't be so damned silly, man! Why, the riotous little devils would hunt every dog on the ground, to say nothing of eating the refreshments—including the committee's meat tea. They'd probably bite a baby or two as well while they're at it. Anyhow, you won't have anyone to whip-in. Jack here will be running in the sports, the parson is sure to find some excuse to be away, and I shall be judging the home-made wine."

"What about Harry the Intendance?"

"If you ask him, he'll say 'my dear sir, I have my official position to consider'."

"Oh, very well, we *won't* have a parade of hounds!"

Dad went out of the backdoor and across the narrow yard into which he released the beagles. Patting heads and black, tan and white bodies, he made hunting noises which set them off baying and yodelling in that charming way beagles have.

Newput Prize Brass Band had been engaged for the afternoon and evening. Colonel Cobley had consented to open the show and all that was needed to make the show one which would go down in the history of Washbrook was fine weather. And fine weather we had. I was well aware of the brilliance of the morning for I awoke with a bellyache that had me out of bed early and writhing on the floor.

The sun was not yet above the ridge of Pharaoh's big barn but its golden light was on the ceiling and half the wall of my small bedroom. Our bantam cock was crowing a challenge and, from the safety of his henhouse, Pharaoh's barnyard rooster was replying, though, if they met in the open, the bigger bird would scuttle for his life.

I knew then that I should never have eaten those dewberries, as we called them. A sort of blackberry but with fewer though bigger berries, they grew low in the hedgerows and, when ripe, had a beautiful blue bloom. They were remarkably sour. Holding my stomach and squirming with pain, I wondered whether Eric and Freddy were suffering as I was. Unashamedly, I hoped they were. After all, we shared most things.

I went out of the back door on bare feet and wearing only a short nightshirt, rather like a mediaeval penitent and in much the same frame of mind. It was then that I remembered I was going to run in the hundred yards race and have a go at the high jump as well. At that moment, I wondered whether I would live as long as the start of the sports! My visit to the little house with its seat for two under the same lean-to roof as the kennels, put me right but started the beagles singing their joyful song which huntsmen love to hear because it tells them that their hounds are healthy and happy.

Whether my father rejoiced at the sound at that early hour I doubted as his red face poked out of an upstairs window. He blinked like an owl at the bright sunlight and bellowed "Quiet, there, *quiet*! Damn the dogs, what are you carrying on at?" I saw him reach beside him where I knew the dressing table stood and then put on his hornrimmed spectacles. "Oh, it's you, boy, is it? Did you have a sudden call?"

"I had an awful guts ache, Dad, but it's gone now."

"Well, there's no point in going back to bed now. Put some clothes on and we'll give the hounds a short walk before breakfast. I've a devil of a lot to do today. It's the show in case you had forgotten." He blinked gratefully at the clear blue sky.

Newput Prize Brass Band, in their scarlet and gold, came in Ernie Spraggin's brake with Ernie himself driving the half-bred cart mare that drew it, and they stopped at the *Cobley Arms* when they came to it. In there also were Turnips and Stumper. Turnips was wearing a little badge on his coat, something to do with him once having gone for a soldier, they said, and now he was a reservist, whatever that might be.

There were two or three others with similar badges and, somehow, they all seemed to walk more upright than before, with shoulders and back braced instead of the rather stooping walk of most farm workers. But the excitement of Show Day were too many for us boys to take much notice of a badge or two.

Dad had to fetch the band, as well as three of the committee, out of the *Cobley Arms*. When they all set off again for Mrs Pyecroft's Home Close, the bandsmen rode in the brake, but Ernie Spraggins said the mare had enough to pull as it was and the others could bloody well walk.

With only ten minutes to go before he was to have opened Washbrook Show, Colonel William Cobley was nowhere to be seen. Dad, with Harry the Intendance, who had said "but of course, my dear sir, anything I can do to help—anything at all," waited at the open gate of Home Close.

The band was sitting on chairs borrowed from Mrs Pawsey or wriggling them on to an even keel on the rough ground. Some of them were making those strange preliminary noises that bands always make before starting on a proper tune.

Poom from a huge, gaping brass thing, *pah* from a lesser one, *pip* from a slender, wooden pipe. There was a lot of unscrewing and shaking of mouthpieces which had been lubricated by beer. The drummer, a squarish man with wide-apart eyes who served behind the counter in Tookey's the grocer's, was fiddling with screws and sometimes giving his instrument a gentle, thudding blow as a promise of worse to come.

Dad kept looking anxiously down the road towards the bend round which was the Grange and then back at the bandsmen hoping they would have their mouthpieces in place and the drumskin tightened in time to welcome Old Billy with music.

From beyond the bend in the road came a swelling drone which even my father's unmechanically attuned ear could not connect with the stutters and bangs of Old Billy's horseless carriage; this was far too smooth.

"My dear sir, here he comes!" exclaimed Harry the Intendance as, a cloud of dust billowing behind and a cheering mob of untidy, small boys running alongside, a shining marvel of engineering skill swung into sight from around the bend. Massive headlamps brassily reflected the rays of the sun, stones flew back from pipe-clayed tyres and *honk, honk*! blurted a brass horn when a gauntletted hand squeezed the rubber bulb.

Dad was thinking that this was far too showy for Old Billy, a decent, modest man, but the sunlight on his spectacles prevented him seeing who rode inside. Perhaps Old Billy had borrowed the vehicle especially for the occasion. My father waved to the expectant bandmaster who flourished his baton and Newput Prize Brass Band crashed into the *March of the Gladiators*.

As the motor car pitched over the undulating field like a boat meeting a head sea, my father told himself that Colonel Cobley would have stopped his motor car just inside the gateway and walked the rest. This one went on until it was right opposite the doors of the tithe barn which, big enough to allow a two-horse wagon to drive in, stood wide open and propped back with baulks of timber.

The arrival of the motor car and its party put a stop to the bickering that was going on inside the barn. This was all to do with the judging of the runner beans. Podger Pike, one of those disturbing men who boast that they always say what they think, had remarked for all to hear that it was mighty queer Poor Arry should win first prize when everybody knew as how he never grew no beans thicker than a bit of bagstring. It was funny, too, that the beans Podger himself had been nursing along with muck and watering just for this very show, were missing from his garden the night before. Mighty queer, it was.

It was then that Arry had been moved to speech beyond his customary "seem'ly." After giving his moustache a more thorough than usual wipe, he had stated his willingness, no chicken though he might be, to take off his coat and give Podger a thump on his big, ugly snout. We boys who had crowded hopefully around were disappointed when the impending fight was postponed indefinitely by the arrival of the motor car and its party.

"Stand back, you children, stand back!" But we took no notice of Little Arriwig as we scuttled out of the barn and surged about the motor, which we saw as part of the programme of entertainment. Alby grinned, Our Nellie stuck her finger in her mouth and we all gawped at the little man in the long, silver-buttoned blue coat and peaked cap who was now holding a door open.

The next to step out of the car was Sir Basil Rossett and I saw the smile leave my father's face as he came hurrying along closely followed by Harry the Intendance. Then, from the rear of the motor and helped down by the chauffeur, out stepped the statuesque Cornelia Cobley and then Lady Basil looking, as Dad afterwards remarked, like a pekinese following a bull mastiff.

They had all lunched uncommonly well at the Grange and Cornelia was feeling almost regal. She held out a hand to my father as if she expected him to kiss it. "How *are* you, Mr Lloyd? And Mrs Lloyd, is she here?" The last question was asked with a glance around as if she had expected Ma to be waiting to receive her with a curtsey. Actually, Ma, who had been tasting home-made wine for the past half-hour, was standing behind the ranks of bottles in the tithe barn and she had just remarked to the village nurse that old Cornelia looked as if she had had a couple herself.

The band had finished with the *Gladiators* and, after shaking their mouthpieces again, were launching into *The Bohemian Girl*. Cornelia had to raise her voice to make herself heard above the din and when she did that it took on a squeak. She had established that my father and the Rossetts had met before and was ransacking her muzzy brain for some other point of contact. She remembered our beagles—those awful little creatures that sometimes chased Poppet, her pom, right up to the front door. "And how are your little doggies?" she asked, forcing a smile.

Dad's own smile returned as he thought of his hounds and the coming beagling season, the "little doggies" part overlooked. "Oh, the hounds are in grand condition, thank you. I hope to get some early morning hunting as soon as the corn is cut and carried. I'm afraid Baggage is in season again, though. May as well have another litter out of her; she always throws good pups. I am thinking of putting her to Mr Butcher's Ranger this time."

I am sure Dad enjoyed the frigid silence that greeted these biological details, but he broke it by asking "Where's the Colonel?" At the same time, he told himself that, under no circumstances was he going to have the show opened by that old humbug Sir Basil.

Cornelia took a deep breath that expanded her full bosom until it strained the whalebone and elastic supporting it and caused her whole superstructure to quiver like an immense jelly. "Colonel Cobley," said she in a ringing voice, "has been called to the Colours!"

"Damn that Kaiser!" exclaimed my father.

"My dear madam," Harry the Intendance had stepped forward, "I expect to be called up myself any day now."

"*You*!" Cornelia Cobley stared at Harry across her vast, lace adorned prow.

Harry the Intendance clicked his heels and stood to attention. "Sergeant, Royal Bucks Hussars, madam!"

Dad looked thoughtful and then said quietly "and I expect I shall enlist too if it isn't over too soon." Then, putting thoughts of war to the back of his mind and recalling the show, he wondered who was to open it. Cornelia settled this question by saying "The Colonel has asked me to perform the opening ceremony—if that is acceptable to you, Mr Lloyd." My father bowed.

I always remembered the date of that show. It was August Bank Holiday, 1914.

CHAPTER TWENTYFOUR

THE SHOW

WE ALWAYS REMEMBERED the day the war started because it was the same as Washbrook Show and *that* was an event we never stopped talking about. The sun went on shining from the time it peeped up over the elms on Hilbury Heights to the moment it slid rosily into the mists around the willows on the river banks.

Long before sunset, however, many important things had happened. Turnips had got drunk enough in the *Cobley Arms* to tell anyone who cared to listen that he, personally, was going to stick a bayonet into the guts of Kaiser Bill. Stumper, slightly less drunk, wished him luck in his admirable resolve if only because the Kaiser had done his best to ruin the Show, the first thing that had ever "gone" in Washbrook. Poor Arry withdrew his moustache from the froth on his beer to remark "seem'ly." The accusation of cheating forgotten—or at least overlooked—he was celebrating winning first prize for runner beans.

Eric Thorne's sister Effie, a couple of inches taller than I was, had her long, golden hair secured by a wide, blue ribbon tied in a big bow. Her eyes were blue too and her fair skin had that transparent look that goes with abounding good health. She was holding a prize for the best bunch of wild flowers. It was a beautiful toy cradle, a miniature of such a one as Joseph of Nazareth might have made for Jesus. Evan Hughes had devoted such care and nearly as much time to its making as he would have done to the real article.

"It's lovely, Effie," I said.

Effie turned the cradle over in her long-fingered hands. "I suppose it's all right. I can give it to our Waggle to put birds' eggs in or something, or perhaps our Mum would like it on the shelf."

Now Little Arriwig was ringing a handbell, the same one he used to summon his pupils back into class when playtime was over.

"Children's sports!" bellowed my father, a little intoxicated himself what with the success of the show and several visits to the *Cobley Arms* to find missing committee men.

Out of the big barn where they had been admiring the runner beans, for which Poor Arry had been given the prize, and Stumper's King Edward potatoes, out of the tea tent, up from their seats on the grass around the band, folks came swarming towards the strip of Widow Pyecroft's Home Close that was now roped off for sports.

The band was busy "polishing the knob on the big front door" for H.M.S. Pinafore, and went on polishing it.

Totsie Varley was there, although she had not shown her face in the village for years except when she cycled through on her way to Newput. She was finished with those trips now and was holding the hand of the reason for the change. The son of Lord What's-is-name was gazing into Totsie's eyes and she had a look on her face that was not unlike that on the faces of other prizewinners.

Although I was standing quite close to them, I did not hear what Dad said to Ernie Spraggins, but I *did* hear the dapper little horse-dealer's reply. "There's nothing like a good, strong outcross in breeding and, by the look of him, the stock could do with improving, even if the dam *is* a bit hairy round the heels. Still, if I'd had anything to do with it, I'd have tried him over a gate first."

There was a bit of grumbling from some of the mothers when I won the hundred yards race by a distance and Old Jinny who, as far as anybody knew, had never been a mother, was heard to say "No wonder they call that Jack Lloyd Spider, him with his long legs! Them others ought to have been given a longer start on him. But what can you expect when his old man is seckertary!"

Finch the gamekeeper was standing beside Dad when I won the race. His calling shouted itself from his fore-and-aft cap, down through the tweed jacket and knickerbockers to the heavy brown boots. As if this were not sufficient proof, sitting beside him was Bracken, the retriever. As I breasted the tape, held by Little Arriwig and Harry the Intendance, a deep rumbling came from Finch's barrel chest. Laughter was a gift which we boys would not have believed to be in the gamekeeper's make-up.

"What's so funny?" my father wanted to know.

"Just that I can see now that if it hadn't been for that weasly little chap with the big boots I could never have got within peppering range of your boy when I came on him and a couple of other young beggars in the Pheasantry!"

My morning bellyache forgotten in the excitement of the sports, I felt an altogether different emotion, one that I found quite delicious, as I watched the girls' skipping race. It was a mixture of the sight of the first flowers in springtime, of a thrush's morning song, of fleecy clouds sailing high in a summer sky, and there was a hint of that strange sensation I had known when I had ducked under Totsie Varley's arm when I went to find Baggage. And they all added up to Effie.

The girls were in their Sunday best frocks, most of them partly covered by starched pinafores; anything less would have been almost indecent. On their feet were high, laced leather boots, made in Olney or Northampton. But the girls themselves had a lean litheness and unbounded energy that came from walking to and from school and from working or playing in the open air when out of school.

Evan Hughes cast up his eyes, clasped his hands and said they resembled angels without wings and wondered why Dad laughed. My own eyes were for Effie only as she came down the course, her golden hair streaming, blue bow dancing, her skipping rope swinging rhythmically.

I thought of a picture I had seen in Alfie Mullard's the Newput antique dealer's window. This was of a lady runner, and while she was running, she was reaching for an apple or something. The lady was wearing considerably less than Effie, but linking the two ideas was almost thrilling. I found myself walking fast through the crowd towards the spot where Effie had just gone through the tape well ahead of all the other girls in the race.

Effie was gnawing an apple that appeared to have been handed to her by Lanky. Her teeth were very white and the juice was running down her chin. Her face was even pinker than before.

"You—you did very well, Effie" I said.

"Ah," said Effie and took another big bite out of the apple. She went on staring steadily at Lanky and there was a peculiar look in her eyes. I walked silently away.

The handbell was being rung again. The bandsmen had shaken their mouthpieces for the last time and were putting their instruments back in their waterproof cases, all except the drummer, who was loosening the skin on his. They seemed to be in a great hurry and, as soon as they had dealt with their instruments, they tucked the lighter ones under their arms and carried the heavy ones at full arm's stretch. Then they joined everybody else as they made their way to the far side of Home Close.

Pharaoh Bugbrooke's pigfloat, with Polly, the patient pony between the shafts, stood there, backed up against a gap in the hedge. Eric, Freddy, Waggle and a swarm of other boys surged towards the float, all keen on having a look at the pig which was to go as prize to the woman of the village who could catch and hold it.

"Stand back, you boys!" cried Little Arriwig, spreading his arms.

"Stand back, d'you hear!" rumbled Finch the keeper, coming to the schoolmaster's aid and holding out his blackthorn stick. "Stand back, or I'll lay this across your behinds!"

But this was no moment to heed the threats of schoolmasters or gamekeepers; this was Show Day and we craned our necks and stood on tiptoe. All we could see of Cronje was a row of long, red bristles sticking up through the mesh of the net that covered the top of the float.

Tiring after a time of wondering about the pig itself, for Pharaoh had kept his secret well, I became aware of heavy breathing behind and above me. Looking round, I saw the spare figure of Chuck Turney and caught a strong, unmistakable whiff of ale.

Chuck was muttering what sounded like a prayer. "Oh, Gawd, let my Aggie win, please let 'er win! If only she wins I swear as I'll never lay a hand on her in anger again!"

"Line up, ladies, please!" On the other side of the hedge, Little Arriwig was stalking up and down the row of runners as if he had been our own bantam cock.

Ernie Spraggins was complaining that there didn't appear to be a very big field of runners and that nobody could call it a maiden race.

"Now, we must all start fair," piped Little Arriwig in the same sort of voice he used when he cautioned one of his pupils. "Mrs Heffer, would you mind stepping back a couple of paces? That's better! Thank you."

Raised voices from some of the onlookers delayed the start. Chuck Turney was threatening Ernie Spraggins who had remarked that it was a pity some of the young 'uns hadn't entered. "What do you think my Aggie is, I'd like to know?" Chuck demanded.

"Well, she's a bit too long in the tooth to be called a filly!"

"I'll ding you one aside the chops!"

"He didn't mean no harm, Chuck." This from Turnips, preceded by a beery burp.

"Shut up, all of you, and let's get on with the race!" growled Stumper whose wife was standing, feet apart, fists clenched, body bolt upright, in the line-up.

Next to the bareheaded Mrs Stumper was Old Jinny, crouched nearly double, rat-trap jaws clenched and black straw hat secured with two dangerous looking hatpins. Sal Heffer was beside her, greying hair screwed into a tight bun, apron (she had been helping with the teas) tucked up and a far-away look on her long, white face.

There was speculation among the spectators as to whether Sal was reckoning up the cost of feeding an extra pig should she be swift enough to overtake it and strong enough to hold it, or whether Evan Hughes was right in his conviction that her thoughts were on the reactions of the late Joe Heffer to this frivolity. And him up there too.

Chuck's Aggie stood three yards clear of Sal Heffer with thoughts only on that gap in the hedge through which Cronje the racing pig was shortly to appear.

Little Arriwig was still fussing along the line of starters. "Now, ladies, you all know the rules of the race. The first one to catch and hold the pig is the winner and she will be entitled to keep it."

"Stand clear of the gap, everybody!" shouted Finch, raising his blackthorn.

"When the pig has got a fair start, I will count three and say '*Go*'!" Little Arriwig announced.

The crowd of onlookers was pushing on to the thorns of the low hedges. The tailboard of the float clattered down and there was a loud squeal from Cronje who was being persuaded to jump out with prods from Pharaoh's stick. A rattle of feet on boards and the pig jumped through the gap in the hedge. There he stood, looking to left and right out of his bright little eyes.

Cronje stood at least two feet and some inches tall and his ginger coloured flanks, all shiny with tallow, were as flat and hard as planks. His upper lip curled over two vicious tusks.

The young hog stuck his toes into the turf and grunted. There he might have remained until nightfall but a sharp thwack on his quarters from Pharaoh's stick made him change his mind.

Giving an angry squeal that might have been heard at Hilbury Heights, Cronje thrust forward his quivering, pink snout, curled his tail tightly (always the sign of a healthy pig) and went forward at a shuffling trot. A loud cheer from the crowd made him shake his ears, squeal again and go into that tireless gallop that he had learned in front of Pharaoh's dogs.

The spectators broke through the gap, we boys in the forefront, and I was reminded of history book pictures of our ancestors hunting the wild boar. Only the spears were missing.

"One, two, three—*go*!" shouted Little Arriwig and the four women hitched up skirts and petticoats and were off like racehorses.

Old Jinny, her nose to the ground like a hunting stoat, her arms working as if they had been piston rods, her whole, scraggy, small body propelled by a scuffling action of her feet, led for the first thirty yards. She was followed closely by Sal Heffer, upright and moving with an effortless swinging stride.

Aggie came next, the lines at the side of her mouth extra deep, her fists held in front of her skinny chest. Last of all came Mrs Stumper, laughing quietly as she moved considerably faster than on her trips to ring the One O'clock Bell, but still with her magnificent hips waggling. She was holding the hem of her skirt high and showing at least twelve inches of stocky leg.

Long Dole, the field next to Home Close on Mrs Pyecroft's farm, and the one where the race had started, is nearly half-a-mile in length and the organisers of the race had not expected the pig to last for more than part of the course. They did not know about Cronje's and Pharaoh's training methods.

At the farther end, Long Dole rises gently in a grassy slope to a stone wall six feet high and another of the boundaries of Parson Blossomville's orchard. The parson himself was not at home, having thought it wiser to dodge the show and what he called its "parish pump politics," by paying a visit to a fictitious aunt whose delicate health served so often as a useful alibi. My father, under bond of secrecy, had told Ma and me of his discovery that an old Boys' cricket match at the parson's old school fell on the same date.

Cronje ran on at a steady, bounding lope. At times he gave a loud squeal to show that he was enjoying himself. Behind, laughing, screaming or just panting according to the nature of each, dashed the women. There were only three of them now in the race. Sal Heffer having been left holding her sides and gasping for breath while she longed to unlace her tight stays in the middle of Long Dole.

Mrs Stumper had slowed down to a fast walk and was still going on simply because she wanted a close-up view of the finish. The laughter was coming from her as she watched Aggie and Old Jinny drawing even further ahead as they ran neck and neck. The pig would have to stop when he came to the wall, that was if one of those two determined women did not catch and hold him before he reached it. But the agile Cronje had a better idea.

The crowd, swarming up the length of Long Dole, we boys well in front, was silent with excitement, except for Chuck who was heard to mutter that the pig would break its bloody neck. Certainly it looked as if Cronje was bent on committing suicide as he raced towards that solid wall without slackening his pace.

Old Jinny's skinny arms were stretched out in front of her, the clawlike hands ready to clutch and hold, when the pig spun round on its hindlegs as nimbly as a polo pony, as Ernie Spraggins put it, slapping his thigh with a riding cane. Old Jinny launched herself at Cronje's flank and sprawled across him, arms about his middle.

For perhaps three seconds, Cronje slowed his pace, encumbered as he was by his would-be captor. It was not because of her weight, which was negligible, it was the way she stuck her toes in the ground which acted as a brake.

Cronje braced himself, flexing his whipcord sinews. Then he cried *oink* and sprang forward like a battering ram propelled by a storming party assaulting a rampart. Old Jinny hung on for ten yards but her grip on the greasy body slipped at the same time that she lost her straw hat and she lay face down on the grass screaming with rage.

A cheer went up from the crowd, for our sympathies were now with Cronje as he galloped towards a thorn hedge and ditch—the same ditch that ran beside Honeymoon Cottage, providing that home with its lavatory flush.

This time Cronje did not even slacken his pace but rose at the low hedge and wide ditch as if he had been a steeplechaser. Again we cheered, and more wildly and loudly still when Aggie, a mane of hair flying behind her, lifted her skirts above her gnarled knees and sprang into the air. Her hairpins had gone at the start of the race and now her hair had shaken loose.

Cronje was over and, though he bumped his knees in landing and grunted angrily, he was quickly up and off again. Aggie cleared the hedge with a foot to spare but she had not allowed for the width of the ditch despite her frequent intimate acquaintance with it.

We heard a splash and saw a shower of water rise above the hedge to scatter itself in spray. Then came the squelching sound of Aggie pulling her feet out of the muddy bottom of the stream, followed by a view of her, now very wet, dashing on into the village street not far behind the tightly curled tail of Cronje.

That same instinct which makes the worker lay down his tools or leave his team to watch a pack of hounds in full cry was alive in most of us and we determined to see the end of this hunt, to be in at the kill.

The hedge and ditch were in front, obstacles which at least three of us would have thought little of when on a poaching expedition. But here, in the full view of farmers, a gamekeeper, and with Long Bob lurking somewhere near the gate, we knew better than to scramble over and through them. Eric, Freddy and I ran back down Long Dole, through the gap, over the showground, through the gateway and out into the street of Down End.

"Don't wait for me!" Freddy panted and, for once, that was a thing neither Eric nor I thought of doing. Past Mrs Perry's shop and round the bend in the road, past the Grange and we came within sight of the pump in the middle of the Knoll. The iron spout was dripping periodically like the tip of Poor Arry's nose and the long handle with its fancy, curly end, was pointed downwards.

The handle seemed to be pointing towards Cronje and Aggie who were sitting side by side close to the pump. Aggie's long arm was round the pig's neck. His eyes were half shut and on his long face with its tusks and whiskers was a look of supreme contentment.

As Aggie laid her cheek against his he gave a happy grunt through a mass of her wet hair.

"Well done, my Aggie!" Chuck Turney had come up behind us "I allus knew as my Aggie could beat the lot of 'em! There ain't nobody like my Aggie!" He glowered about him as if looking for somebody to take up the challenge.

Aggie looked up from the ground where she and Cronje were snuggled together. "And we ain't never going to kill him, not never!"

We turned away from something so very private and went back to the show ground but, after the greasy pig race, any other excitement would have seemed tame that day.

CHAPTER TWENTYFIVE

CHANGE

THE SUN, DROPPING towards the ragged, thatched ridge of the cottage where the Rudd family lived or, at least, went to bed at night, contrived to send some of its golden light through the windows on one side of our own home.

On the dining room floor, I was wheeling a team of Royal Horse Artillery so that they could bring their 12-pounder gun into action against the enemy. A troop of the 12th Lancers was drawn up in front of the sideboard ready to charge after the Horse Gunners had fired off six rounds.

The Queen's Own Cameron Highlanders had rifles levelled (standing, kneeling and lying down, as it said on the box). Over in a corner where the big grandfather clock was ticking, stood the full band of the Grenadier Guards. Some of these were a trifle wobbly considering they were guardsmen; the big drummer, for instance, had his feet set in a dab of plasticine. He had been like this ever since the weight of his instrument had broken him off his lead stand.

Never was a more mixed alliance than that of the enemy. Naked Zulus, shields and spears held high, charged alongside marching French infantrymen and Red Indians brandishing tomahawks. However, they must have possessed a wonderful fighting spirit for some of them were still confronting the opposite side although their own heads were missing.

A glass of dandelion wine in his hand, Dad watched my battle from Baggage's chair. That artful old bitch was shut apart to make sure there was no mistake about her mating before she was sent on her nuptial trip to Mr Butcher's Ranger.

"Boy," said my father "if the Lancers don't charge very soon, that gun and its team are going to be cut off and may have to do what Ramsay's Battery did in the Peninsular War."

"What was that?"

"Limbered up and charged through the Spanish Cavalry without losing a gun or a man." He was silent for a time while I began moving the Lancers. Then he went on "This time, I don't think the war is going to be so spectacular, everybody in drab khaki and so on."

"This time? What do you mean?" Then I remembered the little badges and Old Billy having been "called to the Colours," whatever that meant.

From the little kitchen through the open doorway came sounds of Ma foraging in a drawer for knives and forks and in the cupboard for food. "What is it to be?" she called out, "cold beef, or would you rather have cheese?"

"Leave it to you, Missis. If we eat in the kitchen, we won't disturb this great battle."

Dad always referred to my war games as "this battle" or "the boy's battle," though he would have been more truthful had he called them "our" battles, for he took nearly as much interest in the troop formations, reinforcements and supply columns as I did.

"Who will be in this war, Dad?"

"Turnips and Harry and many more. Colonel Cobley is already in and, before it is over, most of those nice boys whose hands are more used to the plough than the rifle, they will be in too."

Ma called out that supper was ready and I got up off the floor. We went through to the kitchen, my father ducking his head to miss the lintel. That privileged beagle, Dancer, thumped his stern against a table leg as he anticipated the plate-licking to come. On the window seat, Kit the big tabby, stretched his forelegs and stuck out his claws, withdrawing them after a satisfactory examination, and began to purr.

Dad rolled a newspaper and swotted a bluebottle that had buzzed in through the open window. "No telling where it's been. Probably straight off Pharaoh Bugbrooke's dungheap."

"But we are going to win, aren't we?" I asked, pulling a chair from under the table, while Dad sat down on a wide wheelback with strong arms to it. "England always wins, doesn't she?"

"Yes, we will win, but a lot of nasty things will happen before it is all over. Oh, your toy battles are good fun, boy, but make no mistake, real war is horrible—plain horrible."

Ma seemed quieter than usual as she passed the plates and then started cutting bread. She kept looking at Dad in a funny sort of way and, as if to pretend he had not noticed this, father leaned over and patted Dancer's head. He called him a good fellow and rubbed him behind the ears.

"Are you going to be in it too, Dad?"

"In what, boy? Oh, this damned war, I expect so. I must go to Newput Police Station in the morning and see about it."

I had a sudden, peculiar feeling that everything had changed on the day of the village show and that nothing would ever be quite the same again.

The beagle raised his head and looked towards the window. At the same time, the others outside in their kennel started baying. A moment or two later I heard footsteps on the garden path and then the yard gate being opened. Eric and Freddy passed the window on their way to the back door.

"Better go and see what the young monkeys want," said Ma.

I met the two boys outside the door and they had great news. "Freddy has just seen a hare clap in her form on Long Meadow and we reckon that if you could bring one of your dad's beagles we could catch her. Freddy knows where she goes through the hedge into the lane and if he waits in the ditch while we hunt her up, he could nab her!"

Such an unorthodox method of hare hunting would have been frowned on by my father in the ordinary way, especially if it involved one of his hounds, and I knew he must have heard Eric's suggestion.

"It wouldn't take us long," Freddy urged "there's still an hour or two of daylight."

I was surprised when I heard Dad laughing and then his voice. "Take old Dancer here, if you like, but come and finish your supper first."

Things had indeed changed.